WILD IRISH ROSES

In 1922, commemorating the new Irish Free State, illustrator Nell Brinkley drew Kathleen Ni Houlihan as a poor peasant girl and as a queen upon her throne.

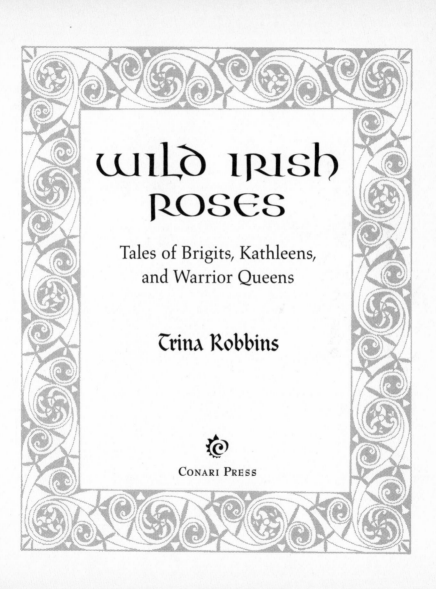

WILD IRISH ROSES

Tales of Brigits, Kathleens,
and Warrior Queens

Trina Robbins

CONARI PRESS

First published in 2004 by Conari Press,
an imprint of Red Wheel/Weiser, LLC
York Beach, ME
With offices at:
368 Congress Street
Boston, MA 02210
www.redwheelweiser.com

Library of Congress Cataloging-in-Publication Data
Robbins, Trina.
Wild Irish roses : tales of Brigits, Kathleens, and warrior queens / Trina Robbins.
p.   cm.
Includes bibliographical references and index.
ISBN 1-57324-952-1 (alk. paper)
1. Women—Ireland—Biography. 2. Ireland—Biography. I. Title.
CT3650.I73R63 2004
920.72'09415—dc22
2004009755

Photographs of Maud Gonne, Countess Markiewicz, and Lady Gregory, and drawing
of Lady Wilde ("Speranza"), courtesy of the National Library of Ireland. Cover of
sheet music for "The Rebel Girl," courtesy of the Labor Archives and
Research Center, San Francisco State University.

Typeset in Aldus

Printed in Canada
MV

11 10 09 08 07 06 05 04
8   7   6   5   4   3   2   1

The paper used in this publication meets the minimum requirements of the
American National Standard for Information Sciences—Permanence of Paper
for Printed Library Materials Z39.48-1992 (R1997).

# CONTENTS

Introduction

You may search everywhere but none can compare to my wild Irish rose.
—Chauncey Alcott, 1899

Poets have personified Ireland as a woman, sometimes calling her the Shan Van Vocht, "the poor old woman"; sometimes Kathleen Ni Houlihan; and sometimes Roisin Dubh, "the little dark rose." This book is a celebration of those roses: tough, independent, and beautiful Irish women who lived between myth and modernity. It spans the centuries from ancient warrior women like Skathach and Aoife, who trained the Irish hero Cuchulain (and were also his lovers), to Countess Markievicz, a warrior for twentieth-century Ireland.

And they're all goddesses! Because the goddesses of ancient Ireland were archetypes—the warrior queen, the *Cailleach* or crone, the muse, or personification of Ireland—and because archetypes are immortal, they've been born over and over again, as women like Countess Markievicz, Maud Gonne, and Mother Jones.

In these pages you'll find Grania O'Malley, notorious sixteenth-century Irish pirate queen, keeping company with literary roses like Lady Gregory, who revived the old Irish heroes and heroines in her writings. I've included one American Beauty Rose: the mythic Scarlett O'Hara. Like her equally mythic warrior ancestress, Queen Maeve, she knew what she wanted and took it.

It was the Irish in her.

About the names: The Irish language was spoken for centuries before it was written down, and when the early Christian monks finally inscribed the words onto parchment, they tossed in as many consonants and vowels as they could. Thus, to an English speaker (or indeed, to anybody but an Irish speaker), ancient Irish names are almost impossible to pronounce. In all cases where the simplified modern spelling is available, I have used it. Medb *has become* Maeve, Granuaile *has become* Grania, *and* Diarmutt *has become* Dermot. *Sometimes I had to choose which spelling to use. In researching* Dervorgilla, *for instance, I found seven other variations of her name:* Devorgill, Derborcaill, Derbhorgill, Derbforgaille, Dervorgoyle, Dearbhfhorgaill, *and* Dearvorgwla!

PART ONE

BEFORE PATRICK

Women were so highly regarded in ancient Ireland that in Irish mythology, the first people to land on Irish soil were fifty women and their queen, Cessair. According to the monks who recorded these stories, Cessair was a daughter of Noah, who wouldn't let her onto his ark, so using an early DIY mentality, she built her own ship and sailed to Ireland. The women brought with them a measly three men, whom they used up pretty quickly. The only surviving man, Fintan, escaped the voracious women by turning into an eagle and witnessing all the rest of ancient Irish history, up to the coming of Saint Patrick. As for Cessair and her women, the flood caught up with them, and they all drowned.

It was a woman who gave Ireland its name. After Cessair and her women, other tribes invaded Ireland, but the last to arrive were the Milesians, ancestors of today's Irish. They found an island already populated with gods and goddesses. As the

Milesian armies progressed across the land, they eventually encountered the goddess Eriu, a woman so powerful that when she threw mudballs down on them from her high hill, the mudballs turned into defending soldiers. However, she foresaw that the Milesians would eventually overthrow her people, the Tuatha De Danaan, so she made a bargain with the Milesians: I'll let your people pass, if you promise to name this island after me. And so they did.

The ancient Irish were a proud Celtic race who loved their singing, loving, and fighting—and the women loved and fought just like the men. They were equal in other ways too: ancient Irish women could be lawyers and judges, could divorce and remarry if they wanted to, and could own their own property. Even into the nineteenth century, they kept their own last names after marriage. As for the fighting part, Irish women often fought side by side with their men, especially when battling Roman invaders. The Romans, who thought of women only as mothers and sex objects, were fascinated by Celtic women warriors, and wrote about them. Diodorus Siculus recorded that "the women are nearly as tall as the men, whom they rival in courage," and Ammianus Marcellinus said that Irish wives were even stronger than their husbands. Warrior queens were so common among the ancient Irish that when the Roman emperor Claudius brought a group of Celtic

Celtic women battle Roman warriors.

prisoners to Rome, they thought Claudius's wife, Agrippina, was the ruler, and they ignored the emperor. For this reason, their mythology was also full of warrior queens like Maeve and the three war goddesses, Macha, Badb, and the Morrigan. And love—ah, love! Old stories tell of aggressive heroines like Dierdre and Grania, who, even though engaged to kings, knew what they wanted—in both cases, much younger and cuter guys—and took it. Even the fierce war goddesses were not immune to love. The Morrigan came on strong to the mythic hero, Cuchulain. When he rejected her, she fought him in the form of a heifer, an eel, and a she-wolf. The battle ended on a draw, with each wounding the other, and the goddess tricked the hero into healing her. The Morrigan's sister, Macha, made the mistake of turning gentle when she fell in love with a human, with bad results for everyone involved.

Most of these mythological stories come from an epic called *Tain Bo Cuailgne*, or *The Cattle Raid of Cooley*, which was Ireland's *Iliad*, *Odyssey*, and *Beowulf* all rolled into one. The stories in the *Tain*, which were first written down by Christian monks in the seventh century A.D., but are hundreds of years older, revolve around a war between Queen Maeve of Connaught and the people of Ulster. While the Greeks fought over Helen, the cattle-loving Irish were fighting over a bull, the greatest bull in Ireland. The Irish Hercules is Cuchulain, a studly warrior who, despite not having much in the brains department, attracted more than his share of wild Irish groupies, including even a goddess or three.

Irish women were not always nice. The warrior queen Aoife exacted a terrible revenge upon Cuchulain when he left her to marry another woman. What the Irish women did to Dervorgilla was just as terrible, and demonstrates that, for all the glamour and romance of the old tales, these people were still primitive and brutally savage.

Warrior Goddesses, Warrior Queens

The Morrigan, Macha, and Badb

According to Irish mythology, the Tuatha De Danaan, a glamorous, godlike race, lived in Ireland before the Celts arrived. After the Celts landed their ships on Irish soil, there was a battle between the Tuatha De Danaan and the Celts, and the Celts won. The Tuatha De Danaan retreated to the island of Tir Nan Og, where they remained forever young, but they also moved into *sidhes,* those fairy hills that dot the Irish landscape, and the Irish people named them the Sidhe, after their hills. They continued to interact with the new, mortal inhabitants of Ireland for hundreds of years, even after the church demoted them to the status of fairies.

Like the Irish themselves, the Sidhe loved to fight and loved to love. Among their minions were three warrior-goddess sisters, Macha, Badb, and the Morrigan. The bloodthirsty three would take on the shape of ravens and fly above the scenes of battle, shrieking battle cries and egging their people on to victory.

Badb was the banshee, wailing over the dying. She was also the ominous Washer at the Ford, who predicted death. Sometimes a warrior who was doomed to fall in battle would see Badb as a beautiful young woman, weeping while she washed out bloody

clothing in a river or stream. Then he would realize with horror that the bloody clothing was *his.*

All three sisters could morph into ravens, ancient crones, or comely young women. It was in the latter guise that they usually emerged from their hills to have a fling with whatever strapping young human stud caught their eye.

As did so many human women in those days, the Morrigan found herself attracted to the hero, Cuchulain, who preferred war to love and rebuffed her. Of course, it's bad luck to spurn a goddess, as Cuchulain learned. The angry goddess came against him in battle, and when the dust settled, both of them were the worse for wear.

Eventually the two became friends. Before Cuchulain's last battle, the Morrigan even tried to keep him from getting himself killed by breaking the shaft of his chariot. Cuchulain, too proud to pay attention, and also a little dim, ignored the warning and went to his death. And when he died, the Morrigan, in the shape of a crow, flew down and perched on his shoulder.

Being a natural troublemaker, maybe because she loved fighting so much, the Morrigan was also a cattle rustler. The ancient Irish held cattle to be so important that they counted their wealth in cows, and were forever stealing each others' herds. Once the Morrigan stole a cow belonging to a mortal woman named Odras, and tried to take it into her fairy hill. When Odras tried to get her cow back, the goddess turned the unfortunate woman into a pool of water.

The Morrigan outdid herself when she stole a magical cow of the Sidhe to mate with the great brown bull of Cooley. With this act, she put into motion the events that caused the great war between Ulster and Connaught known as the Cattle Raid of Cooley.

After mating the two animals, the Morrigan returned the cow to its fairy hill, and in due time the cow gave birth to a magical, talking calf. Shortly after that, the Sidhe went to war against the king and queen of Connaught, Ailill and Maeve. In the heat of battle, the fairy calf met and fought with Ailill's prize bull, the white bull of Connaught. Young upstart that he was, the calf lost the battle with the bull, and cried out, "If my father, the great brown bull of Cooley, was here, he'd beat you from Connaught to Ulster!" For the two bulls had been enemies before they were even born; they were reincarnations of two men of the Sidhe who had been sworn enemies in life.

When Maeve heard those words from the mouth of the remarkable calf, she exclaimed, "By the Goddess, I will neither eat, nor drink, nor will I sleep, until I see the great white bull fight the great brown bull!" Whereupon she tried to get the brown bull from its owner, and when he wouldn't give it up, she went to war with him and with all the people of Ulster.

All of this was the fault of the Morrigan, who, being a goddess, could foresee the future and knew darn well that she would cause a war.

For the Morrigan, love and war went together like a horse and carriage. One Samhain eve, before a great battle, the Dagda, king of the Tuatha De Danaan, strolled by the banks of the river Unius and ran into the Morrigan, who was bathing in the river. Naked and magnificent, with the nine locks of her hair unloosed, she stood with her right leg on one side of the river and her left leg on the other side (they were giants in those days).

The sight of her inflamed the Dagda, and as for the Morrigan, she never needed to be asked twice. The two of them went at it, then and there, on the grassy banks of the river, beneath the starry sky of Ireland. The Dagda must have been really good in bed, because the Morrigan was so delighted by his performance that she promised him victory in the next day's battle—and she had the power to do that.

Sure enough, the Tuatha De Danaan won the war. Then the Morrigan committed a gruesome act that reminds us just how long ago these tales were first told, and how savage were the people who told them. She scooped up two handsful of blood from the enemy dead and gave it to her tribe to drink!

No matter how much she lusted after some guy, the Morrigan was *never* nice. Her sister Macha, on the other hand, who was so nasty that the heads of warriors cut off in battle were called "Macha's acorn crop," made the mistake of sacrificing her fierce nature when she fell in love with the mortal, Crunden. Crunden was a poor but handsome widower, who lived in a lonely cottage in the Ulster hills. In her attempt to become the kind of woman he might go for, Macha gentled herself into a mortal woman. In the form of a beautiful woman, she marched through the astonished man's door one day, and commenced to make up the fire. She then swept the dust bunnies off the messy floor (Crunden, no house-keeper, had let his home go to seed), milked the cow, and whipped up some tasty oat cakes, all without saying a word. He must have thought he had died and gone to heaven, because that night she climbed into his bed, too. He awoke the next morning to discover she'd already chopped the wood, rounded up the cattle, shod his horse, and prepared him a steaming bowl of porridge.

They lived together happily after that. Crunden was too delighted with his good luck to ask questions, and anyway, Macha didn't supply any answers, because she never said a word. She must have eventually started to talk, though, because one day there was to be a big fair in Ulster, and Crunden announced his intention to go.

"Don't do it," she said.

"And why not?" he whined. "All the other guys are going. If I don't go, they'll say I'm henpecked."

Macha sighed. Men could be such children! "Go then," she said, "but at least promise not to mention me to anyone."

"No problem," said Crunden. And he went to the fair.

The most exciting part of the fair was always the annual char-iot race, and this time it was won by the king's own stallions. While listening to the poets and minstrels praising the royal horses, Crunden couldn't keep his big mouth shut. He'd seen his wife perform some remarkable feats, and though she had told him nothing about her past, he knew that she was no ordinary woman.

So he spoke up. "That's nothing. My wife could outrun those horses."

There was a sudden silence, and everyone turned to stare at him. Already Crunden regretted having spoken. The king ordered, "Seize that man."

When the king's guards arrived at her cottage door, somehow Macha was not surprised. She knew that she shouldn't have let that handsome lout go anywhere by himself.

"What kind of trouble has he gotten himself into?" she asked.

"You'd best come with us," they replied.

Macha was nine months pregnant, but she gathered up her skirt, threw a shawl over her shoulders, and followed the guards to the fair, where the king and all the people waited for her.

"This man"—the king pointed to Crunden, cowering wretchedly in chains—"said that you could outrun my prize horses. Is this true?"

"And what if I can?" replied Macha.

"Then you must do it now," said the king. "Or your husband dies."

Macha threw off the shawl and displayed her big belly. "How can I run now, and me being nine months with child?" She demanded, "Have pity on me, and at least wait until my baby is born."

"Then put the man to the sword," ordered the king.

Macha appealed to the watching crowd. "Help me, people of Ulster, for every man of you had a mother."

But the crowd stood silent, waiting for the big show, and there was nothing to do but to race, pregnant as she was. Macha outran the horses, of course—after all, she was a goddess—but at the finish line she sank to her knees in the dirt and gave birth to twins, a boy and a girl. Goddess or not, she was in great pain, and screamed in her labor, and as soon as they heard her scream, all the men of Ulster were overcome with labor pains.

Macha cursed them. "For nine generations, you men of Ulster shall pay for what you did to me. When you most need your strength, when you're threatened by enemies, you'll be weak as a woman with child, and suffer the pangs of childbirth."

Thus the ancient capitol of Ulster, where this story took place, was called *Emain Macha*, or "the Twins of Macha." Some sources say that Macha died after this, but, as she was a goddess, that's pretty unlikely. No one recorded what happened to her babies. I think she left them with Crunden and departed in a huff to her fairy hill, vowing to have nothing more to do with mortal men.

THE OTHER MACHA

If we are to believe the monks who recorded Irish history in the seventh century, there was also a flesh-and-blood Macha, who lived in the fourth century. She was a warrior queen, and because of her flame-colored hair she was called Macha Ruadh, or Macha the Red. Her father, Aedh, was one of three brothers who took turns at ruling Ireland for seven years each. When all three king had served their terms, Aedh died, and Macha claimed his turn at the throne as her birthright. Her two uncles, Dithorba and Cimbaoth, refused to let her rule because she was a woman, so Macha solved the problem by marrying Cimbaoth and going to war against Dithorba. Defeating Dithorba, she ruled for seven years until another problem popped up: Dithorba's sons, now grown, wanted the throne for themselves.

Fiery as her hair, Macha was not one to give in. Disguised as a leper, she went looking for the five sons. She found them sitting around a campfire in the forest, after a day of hunting. Macha's beauty must have shone through her disguise, because leper or not, after sharing their food with her, one by one the brothers took her into the forest with sex on their minds. What they got was overpowered and trussed up like pigs, while Macha went to fetch the next brother. Then she dragged the lot of them back to Ulster, where she forced them to build a fort for her.

Macha unfastened the brooch that held her cape, and with its pin, she marked out the boundaries of the fort she wanted built. Thus, goes the story, her fort was called *Emain Macha*, or "Macha's brooch." You have your choice of etymologies for the phrase.

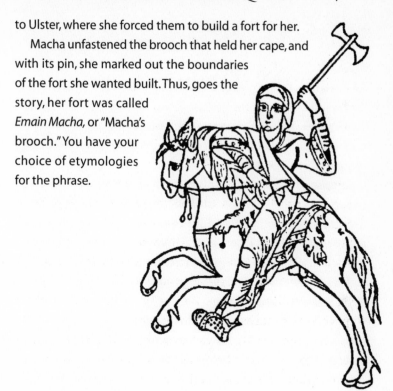

Maeve and Findabair

Maeve, the scandalous queen of Connaught in ancient Ireland, was a warrior queen. In her gilded chariot she led her people to battle against the men of Ulster during that great war called the Cattle Raid of Cooley. Findabair was Maeve's lovely daughter. Maeve was no slouch in the looks department herself, as her many lovers would have told you, and she was a fierce woman, used to being in control. She certainly lorded it over her henpecked husband, King Ailill, telling him that no husband of hers could be jealous, because she always had one man in the shadow of another. Ailill knew full well that he was king only because of Maeve, for she had been married three times before, and each of her husbands had owed their kingship to her. You couldn't be king in Connaught unless you were married to Maeve.

It was hard enough for Findabair to have such a domineering mother, because this beautiful princess—her name meant Fair Brow—was also a feisty gal. But it was worse when Maeve tried to meddle in her daughter's love life.

Froech was only half-mortal. His mother was one of the Sidhe, the godlike fairy folk of Ireland, and she had given her son a gift

of twelve red and white cows from the shadow world. In a land where cattle were highly valued and cows were even worshipped as goddesses, these cows were very special. They gave the sweetest milk in all of Ireland.

Findabair had heard tales of Froech's beauty, and she fell in love with him without ever having seen him. She talked to the right people, who talked to the right people, and word got to Froech that the daughter of Queen Maeve was in love with him. He loaded his chariots with gifts of gold and silver and precious stones, and, with his men and horses and hounds and harpers, set out for Maeve's castle in Connaught.

When the people of Connaught saw Froech and his band coming up over the hill to the castle, all that gold and silver dazzled their eyes. But Maeve's eyes were especially dazzled by the handsome young Froech, and after graciously accepting his gifts, she pulled out her golden chessboard with silver chess pieces, and invited him to play. They played chess without stopping for three days and three nights, and Froech was careful to let Maeve win every game.

Finally, Maeve returned to her senses, and called for meat and drink. After three straight days of chess, she was starving, and, holding a joint of venison in one hand and a drinking horn brimming with ale in the other, she got around to asking the purpose of Froech's visit.

"I've come to ask for the hand of your daughter," replied Froech.

Maeve was disappointed. She had wanted this magnificent specimen for herself, so she slumped back in her throne, sulked, and said nothing. Finally, Ailill spoke up. "You can have Findabair if you pay the bride price I ask."

"Name your price, "said Froech.

Ailill was feeling greedy. After all, he reasoned, this part-fairy suitor should be able to give them anything they wanted. So he said, "Sixty gray horses with gold bridles, and your twelve red and white cows, with a white calf for each cow, and all your men and musicians to aid us in our battle with Ulster." For Maeve and Ailill were already preparing for war.

Froech was appalled. "I wouldn't give that much for Maeve herself," he exclaimed, and stomped out of the hall.

Froech walked down to the river to calm himself, and who should be bathing in the water but fair Findabair? He immediately recognized her, because only Maeve's daughter could be so lovely, and she of course knew by his otherworldly beauty that he must be Froech.

"Your father's giving me a hard time," he told her. "Let's just run away together."

"Run away with you indeed," cried Findabair. "And I a king's daughter? It's a proper wedding we'll have, as befits a princess, the finest Ireland has ever seen. Don't worry, Daddy will come around. And meanwhile, here's a token of my love."

She took a gold ring off her finger and gave it to him. "It was a gift from Daddy, but if he asks, I'll say I lost it."

They didn't know that, watching from the topmost tower of the castle, Ailill could see his daughter take something shiny off her finger and give it to Froech, who put it into the leather pouch he wore on his belt. He had a pretty good idea as to what it was.

"Our daughter gave that boy my ring," he told Maeve. "She's going to run off with him, and we'll be disgraced."

"Then we'll simply have to kill him," replied the ever-practical Maeve.

The next day Maeve and Ailill acted like nothing had happened. Along with Findabair, they took Froech hunting. Around noon, they escaped the heat of the day by resting in the cool shadows of a grove of trees that grew around a dark lake in the forest. Maeve said, "I hear you're a good swimmer, Froech. I would love a branch of those red berries that are growing there, on the other side of the lake. Will you get them for me?"

Maeve knew that a serpent lived in the lake, an Irish version of the Loch Ness Monster. Clueless Froech stripped and jumped into the water. Findabair, watching, had never in her life seen anything as beautiful as his perfect body, and she resolved that, no matter what her parents tried, she wouldn't let him come to harm. As Froech swam to the other side of the lake, Ailill picked up his leather pouch, shook out the ring, and tossed it into the water. He turned away then, and didn't see a big salmon leap from the water and swallow the ring, but Froech did, and he caught the salmon in his hands and hid it under some bushes by the lakeside. Then he swam back with a branch of berries, which he presented to Maeve.

Disappointed that the monster hadn't shown up, Maeve gave it one more try. She finished the berries and exclaimed, "These berries were so delicious! Could you bring me just one more branch?"

Doing his best to make Findabair's mother happy, Froech jumped into the water again. This time he was out of luck; the monster surfaced and attacked him. Froech, wrestling with the monster, called out, "A sword! A sword!" but none of the king's men dared help him, so they just stood there in silence. Not so Findabair. Quickly she pulled off her clothes, and, sword in her teeth, dove into the water and swam as close as she dared. She tossed the sword to Froech, who sliced off the monster's head and carried it to shore.

But Froech was badly wounded, and now Maeve and Ailill began to regret what they had done. "If he dies," murmured Maeve to Ailill, "the Sidhe will rise up against us, and we have no power against their magic." So they soaked Froech in a bath of healing herbs, and put him to bed wrapped in bandages of clean linen.

It didn't look good for Froech. Maeve sent for her druids, who predicted that the wounded youth wouldn't last the night. Findabair was heartbroken and furious; she would never forgive her parents if her true love died. But then the people of Connaught heard a loud weeping outside the city walls, and there were fifty women of the Sidhe, clothed in scarlet and silver, each more beautiful than the last. They had come for Froech.

The fairy women bore Froech away on a silver stretcher, and returned him the next night, healed and without a scar on him. Maeve and Ailill welcomed him back and pretended that it had all been an unfortunate accident, but of course Findabair knew better. Ailill muttered to his wife, "Now what do we do? It would seem that the fairy youth is invincible."

Calmly, Maeve replied, "Well if we can't kill Froech, we'll just have to kill Findabair."

Now, Maeve and Ailill were in the habit of counting their wealth. In fact, one version of the Cattle Raid of Cooley says that it started because once, when they counted their belongings, Maeve found that she had one less bull than Ailill, and to make up for it she had to steal the prize bull of Cooley. So the next evening, nobody was surprised when Ailill declared that he wanted all his treasures brought to him at dinner, so that he could count them. Froech, though, had an inkling of what this might be leading up to, so he called aside one of his men and told him, "Go to the lake where I fought the monster. Under a bush by the lakeside you'll find a salmon that I left there. Take it to Findabair and have her cook it. She'll know what to do with it."

That night the candles burned brightly at the dinner table, but even brighter shone the mountain of gold and precious stones that made up Ailill's riches. The king turned to his daughter and said, "There's only one more item that I need to complete this collection, and that's the gold ring I gave you. May I have it back to place on top of all my treasures?"

Findabair looked down. "I—I'm afraid I lost it, Daddy," she said.

"Lost it? Well, that won't do! You'll have to find what you lost, or it'll be your life that's lost."

The king's men and the queen's ladies were horrified. "Surely," they exclaimed, "you wouldn't take your daughter's life over a little thing like a gold ring?"

But the king was adamant. "That was a very special ring. Find it," he ordered his daughter, "or lose your head."

Findabair shouted, "I swear by the Goddess that if I find that ring, I'm out of here as soon as I can find a man to take me."

Ailill sneered. He knew the ring was in the middle of the pool. "You'll never find that ring, but if you do, you can elope with the stableboy for all I care."

And Findabair signaled to her maid, who ran off to the kitchen. She returned carrying a covered golden dish, which she set in front of Findabair. Findabair removed the cover, and there lay the salmon, still steaming, and on top of it was the gold ring.

"Hmmm," said Ailill. There was nothing for it but to grant his daughter's wishes and let her marry the brave and handsome man she'd set her cap for.

As for Maeve, she sat and sulked, and said nothing.

FINDABAIR'S UNHAPPY ENDING

Before Froech and Findabair could marry, the great war with Ulster began, with disastrous results. Froech fought on the side of Maeve, as he had promised, and drowned early on. Meanwhile, Maeve, trying to find men who would be willing to take on the Ulster champion, Cuchulain, in hand-to-hand combat, promised each warrior that if he fought Cuchulain, he could have Findabair. Of course, Findabair never had an inkling that she was being offered as incentive to fight. For such a reward, each warrior willingly fought Cuchulain, only to get slaughtered. Then Maeve would find another innocent young soldier and promise Findabair to *him,* in order to get him to fight Cuchulain. That guy would get slain, too, and she'd find yet *another* sucker. This went on until Findabair, still mourning her dead lover, got wind of it. Horrified that her mother was offering her to every soldier in their army, she died of shame.

Skathach of Skye and Aoife of Alba

Skathach, the warrior queen, stood on the battlements of her fortress on the Shadowy Island, surrounded by 150 scarlet-cloaked warrior handmaidens. She looked down at the teenaged Irish boy who was trying to cross the Bridge of Leaps. This was the high, narrow footbridge that connected her island to the mainland, and crossing it wasn't easy. It was a magic bridge, and if you stepped on one end, the bridge might rise up and fling you right back upon land. On the other hand, if you tried to jump onto the middle—well, it was very narrow, and a miss would send you into the boiling waves below. Anyone who made it across the bridge earned the right to be accepted by Skathach and trained in the arts of fighting. Near the bridge was an encampment of wannabe warriors who had hoped to reach her for training, only to be turned back by the bridge.

Twice the young man stepped onto the bridge and was tossed back onto land. The small group of warrior-rejects laughed and jeered at him. The third time he made a running jump, landed smack dab in the center of the bridge, bounced once and somersaulted onto the other end. Skathach was impressed. This young man, Cuchulain, had proven that he was worthy of being her student. Besides, with his black hair and bright blue eyes, he was a good-looking hunk of guy. Skathach, who was nearly twenty years older than Cuchulain, impressed him, too. With her perfectly conditioned body clad in shining armor and her auburn hair cropped short like a warrior, she was a sight such as he had never seen before, and for the time being he forgot all about his dainty sweetheart Emer, who was the reason he had come there in the first place. She had refused to marry him until he became a great warrior.

Cuchulain lived and learned with Skathach until she could teach him no more, in more ways than one. During the day they fought, and at night they made love. Cuchulain was a good student, and when a year and a day had passed, she presented him with the Gae Bolg, a magic sword that could not miss, and that always killed. The sword would be the cause of a great tragedy some day, but Cuchulain couldn't have known that when he accepted it.

Skathach had a younger sister, Aoife, who was also a warrior queen. In fact, because she knew magic, she was the greatest warrior in the world, and no one had yet beaten her in battle. The two sisters were rivals, and it finally reached the point where they declared war on each other. When Cuchulain saw Skathach buckling on her armor, he shouted, "A fight! Let's go!"

No way, thought Skathach, this impetuous boy will just get

himself killed. And she spiked his drink before departing for the battle alone, leading her soldiers. The powerful drug would have knocked out any ordinary person for a night and a day, but Cuchulain was no ordinary person. He woke up in an hour, realized his queen had gone on without him, and ran after the war party, quickly catching up with them.

The day of battle dawned bright and sunny, and Aoife challenged her sister to meet her on a mountaintop for single combat. Cuchulain put out his hand to stop Skathach, who was already striding forward, sword held high. "Wait!" he cried. "It would be wrong for sister to slay sister. Let me fight her instead. I ask only one thing: What does Aoife love most in the world?"

"Easily answered," replied Skathach. "Her horse and chariot, and her chariot driver."

Cuchulain raced up the mountain to where Aoife waited, her copper-colored hair loose and shining in the morning sun. She was even more beautiful than her sister. Truly, he thought, it would be a shame to have to kill her.

Shouting battle cries, the two warriors attacked each other fiercely, but Aoife was the better warrior, and soon she had shattered Cuchulain's sword and spear. Resorting to trickery, he pointed behind her, shouting, "Look! Your horse and chariot, and your chariot driver, have fallen over the cliff!"

Cuchulain battles Aoife.

Aoife spun around to look, and Cuchulain seized her, threw her to the ground, and held his knife to her throat. He made her surrender, and promise she would never fight her sister again. Aoife took a fancy to this dark-haired youth who had tricked her into defeat, and when she returned to Alba, she took him with her. Skathach didn't mind. She was growing tired of the wild boy anyway. Cuchulain stayed with Aoife and learned more of the arts of love and war from her.

Then one day it was time to leave. Before Cuchulain left, Aoife told him that she was pregnant with their child. Cuchulain gave her a gold ring for the baby. "If you have a boy, "he told her, "as soon as he is grown enough so that this ring fits his finger, send him to me in Ireland."

Cuchulain never told Aoife about Emer waiting for him back home, and that was a mistake. Aoife raised their son, Connla, to be a great warrior, but when she heard that Cuchulain had taken a wife, she grew furious. She sent Connla off to find Cuchulain, but first she put upon him a *geisa*. To the ancient Irish, a geisa was a kind of holy vow, curse, and taboo, all rolled into one. To disobey your geisa was to invite terrible retribution from the gods themselves, so you just didn't do it. And this is what she told him: "You must never tell your name to any man, even if you have to fight them all and kill them."

Connla sailed to Ulster, the home of his father, and when the men of Ulster asked his name, he refused to give it. So they fought him, one by one, and he killed them all, until no one was left standing but Cuchulain, the champion of Ulster. The two were evenly matched, which is no surprise, since they were both trained by the same woman. Finally, as he had with Aoife, Cuchulain cheated: he drew from its sheath the Gae Bolg, his magic sword that never missed and that always killed, and he slew the boy who was his own son.

Sometimes Celtic women took a terrible revenge.

CELTIC REVENGE

Ancient Irish women excelled in cruel revenge. Sin (her name is pronounced *Sheen)* lived in the days when Christianity had recently come to Ireland, but not all the saints in the land could keep her from using magic, because she was an enchantress. Muirchertach, the high king of Ireland, had killed her family, so she vowed to destroy him.

One day, when Muirchertach was riding through a forest, Sin just happened to be in his path. She was not hard on the eyes anyway, but Sin had enchanted herself to be the most irresistible creature the king had ever seen, and he instantly fell hopelessly in love with her. He dismounted and took her by the lily white hand.

"Who are you, fairest maiden?" he breathed.

"Easily told," she replied. "But you must never say my name. I am Storm, Rough Wind, Winter Night, Cry, Wail, and Groan."

The king was horrified at the string of terrible names she uttered, but then she fluttered her lashes and added, "I am also King Muirchertach's mistress."

The king was delighted. "Then come live with me at my palace."

"But don't you have a wife? And children?"

"Well, yes, but …"

"Dump them. And your priest, too. If you really want me, no man of the church can be in the same room with me."

The smitten king did as he was told. He tossed out his wife and children, and sent away all his priests. In return, Sin consented to sit at his right side on the throne.

"Are you a goddess?" he asked her.

"I'm just a daughter of Eve, but I can perform magic," she told him, and made wine from water, and pigs from ferns. Muirchertach drank the wine and ate the pork, and it was delicious, but it sapped his strength and made him weak as a baby.

Now Sin commenced to torment the king by conjuring up illusions of demon hordes attacking the palace. Weak as he was, Muirchertach took up his sword and ran out to fight them, but he thrust his sword through nothing but mist and smoke. Finally, on the eve of Samhain, the Celtic Halloween, she conjured up the mother of all storms. Terrified by the screaming wind, the king tried to calm himself by saying, "It's just a winter storm."

"Storm is my name, O mortal," she replied. "Why do you say my name? Now you are truly doomed."

The king sighed, "I know. I was doomed the moment I met you."

Now Sin conjured up flames to attack the palace. Muirchertach tried to flee, but the place seemed to be surrounded by ghastly armies.

Sin led the dazed king to a vat of wine. "In here," she said, "you'll be safe from the fire."

As the king climbed into the vat, he begged, "At least tell me who you are!"

Muirchertach sank into the deep vat of wine, and as the liquid closed over his head and he drowned, the last words he heard were Sin, screaming, "I am Sin, the enchantress, whose family you killed, and this is my revenge!"

They Knew What They Wanted

Deirdre

Arranged marriages were not forced on the women of ancient Ireland. Women were free to pick and choose their husbands, to accept and reject whomever they chose. Unfortunately, that freedom didn't amount to a hill of beans if the suitor happened to be a king. And that's what caused Deirdre, known as Deirdre of the Sorrows, to become the most tragic heroine of Irish legend.

Conor Mac Nessa, high king of Ulster, liked to have his way, and woe to anyone who crossed him. One day Conor was visiting the house of his storyteller, Felim Mac Dall. Felim's pregnant wife was serving the king and his company when suddenly her unborn baby cried out from the womb. Amazed, and worried about this portent, Conor sent for his druid, Cathbad, to come and explain what had happened.

Cathbad laid his hands on the woman's stomach and announced, "This girl child who is to be born will be the fairest in all of Ireland, and her name will be Deirdre. But she brings bad luck, war, and sorrow. Brave men will die because of her."

Conor's men were horrified. They cried, "Kill the baby now!"

But Conor was intrigued. He had already been married to the infamous Queen Maeve, but his union with the headstrong queen had been a disaster. Now he had no wife. He commanded that the baby be taken from her parents and brought up in secrecy and isolation far from Ulster, where nobody would see her, and she would see nobody. Her only companions would be an old man to do the heavy work, and the poetess Levarcham to be her foster mother and teacher. And when she was old enough, Conor would marry her.

Deirdre grew up to be as beautiful as Cathbad had predicted. Word of her beauty was carried to Conor, who started planning the wedding. One winter day when she was a teenager, Deirdre watched her old manservant slaughter a calf for dinner. The calf's blood spotted the snow, and a raven flew down to drink the blood.

Deirdre, who had never seen any man but her old servant, remarked to Levarcham, "It's strange, but I had a dream about a man whose skin was as white as the snow, whose hair was as glossy and black as the raven's wing, and whose lips and cheeks were as red as that calf's blood. But of course that's silly. No man like that exists—*does* he?"

"There is indeed a man like that," replied the poetess, who hated to see Deirdre marry an old king. "His name is Naoise, and he's one of the three sons of Usnach. And I can show you where to find him."

Levarcham took Deirdre to the hills behind Ulster, where Naoise lived with his brothers. Naoise stood outside his house, counting his cattle. When Deirdre emerged from behind the cows and ambled over to him, he raised an eyebrow and said, "Now there's a fine heifer."

"Heifers are always fine," retorted Deirdre, "when there are no bulls around."

Although he had never seen her, Naoise knew that this strange but lovely girl must be Deirdre. Everyone in Ulster knew about the beautiful young woman whom King Conor kept hidden away, so he said, "But you're promised to the biggest bull of all, King Conor."

"Hah!" Deirdre snapped her finger. "I don't give *that* for the old king! I want a young bull."

Naoise knew he was in dangerous territory, because one simply did not risk the anger of Conor Mac Nessa. He turned to leave, but Deirdre grabbed him by his ears and laid upon him a geisa, the strange Irish combination of prayer and curse, that could not be disobeyed.

"May these two ears be ears of shame and derision if you don't run away with me right now," she said.

So Naoise ran off with Deirdre, and he didn't have to think twice about it. His faithful brothers, Ardan and Ainle, came with him, and the four of them lived in the forests, eating the deer that the brothers killed and the salmon they caught. Conor, of course, was furious, and sent his men after them, so Deirdre and the three

Dierdre meets Naoise.

brothers escaped to Scotland, where Naoise and his brothers swore allegiance to the Scottish king, to serve him and to protect him. In return he gave them land next to Loch Ness, where they built a small cottage. But the Scottish king didn't know about Deirdre, because the brothers kept her secret. They knew too well that her beauty could get them all in trouble.

One day the king needed Naoise and his brothers to fight for him, so he sent a messenger to them. The messenger came upon Naoise and Deirdre, sitting in front of their cottage, playing chess. Deirdre hurried inside when she saw the messenger, but it was too late. He had already seen how her hair glistened like gold in the sun, how her blue eyes sparkled like the lakes of Scotland, and how her lips were redder than the berries that grew in the forest. He returned to the king with his news.

"I've just seen the most beautiful maiden in this land, and in any other land," he said. "And she's living next to Loch Ness with Naoise and his brothers. She'd be better off as your wife."

The king pondered this. If he tried to claim this marvelous woman, the brothers would fight to defend her, and they were good fighters. Besides, it wouldn't look good for a king to steal the wife of the man who had claimed refuge with him. Best to be subtle, he decided.

After this, the king sent the brothers out on the front lines whenever there was a battle, hoping they'd be dispatched by the enemy, and he'd have the job of consoling Naoise's widow. Miraculously, the brothers survived three such battles with mere scratches, but soon they realized what the king had in mind for them, so they packed up and left.

Deirdre and the sons of Usnach then went to Queen Maeve, who gladly took them in. Any enemy of her ex-husband was her friend. But Maeve hated to be outshone, and next to Deirdre, her beauty faded away like dew in sunshine. Deirdre, Naoise, and his brothers were growing more and more uncomfortable in Maeve's court, when word reached them that Conor had forgiven them and was inviting them back to Ulster. The trusting sons of Usnach were delighted, and started packing.

Deirdre warned them, "Don't go. I have a very bad feeling about this."

Naturally, they ignored her, and of course when they reached Ulster, Conor's men were waiting for them with swords and spears. All three brothers were slain, and it was Conor's best man, Eogan Mac Durthacht, who killed Naoise. Deirdre was taken to Conor's palace to live with him, but for a year and a day she never smiled or even raised her head, so full of sorrow was she.

At the end of the year, Conor asked her whom she hated the most, and she answered, "You and Eogan Mac Durthacht."

"So that's the way it is, "said he. "You'll be spending a year with Eogan and a year with me." And he bound her hands, and placed her in his chariot to be taken to her lover's killer. Along the way, the chariot passed between two tall standing stones, and Deirdre hurled herself from the chariot and dashed her brains out on one of the stones.

Deirdre was buried next to Naoise, and a tall pine tree grew from her grave. Another pine grew from the grave of Naoise; the two trees intertwined high in the sky, and nothing would part them.

GEISA 101

The geisa figures in a great many early Irish story, and is a handy plot device. If you disobeyed your geisa, you were always doomed. Sometimes you had two contradictory geisas, and that would mean the end of you. Cuchulain, whose name meant "Hound of Culain," had a geisa put on him that said because of his name, he could never eat dog. On the last day of his life, he came upon three old crones sitting around a fire, cooking a dog, and they invited him to join them and share their food. Unfortunately for Cuchulain, he had another geisa that said that he could never refuse an offer of hospitality, so he shared the dog, and in the end, that caused his death.

The power to lay a geisa on someone seems to have come in handy with women who had their eye on certain men. Deirdre and Grania each used geisas to get their reluctant Mister Right to run away with them.

Grania

Two centuries after Deirdre ended her tragic life, King Cormac ruled Ireland, and the legendary hero Finn Mac Cool was his general. Finn led a group of elite warriors called the Fennians, who were a kind of ancient Irish national guard and knights of the round table combined. Only the greatest athletes and warriors were fit to join the Fennians, and Irish lore is full of their exploits.

Finn was an aging warrior when he decided it was time for him to marry, and King Cormac offered his own daughter, the princess Grania, as a wife. In all fairness, it must be noted that Grania had agreed to marry Finn, for in those days women still had the right to make up their own minds. But Grania had no idea that the famous hero Finn Mac Cool was now an old man. She realized this when Finn showed up for the engagement party, along with his Fennians. Bringing his Fennians with him was a big mistake, for right after the disappointed Grania saw that she was engaged to a geezer, she set eyes on Finn's captain, Dermot.

Dermot was sometimes called Dermot of the Love Spot, because he had a beauty mark on his cheek that made him irresistible to the female sex. The rest of him, all curly black hair and blue eyes and muscles, was not bad, either. Grania did what any smart

Grania lays a geisa on Dermot.

princess would do in the same situation: she spiked everyone's ale except Dermot's. When the entire company was snoring loudly, she declared her love to the handsome young man with the love spot. When Dermot was reluctant to cross his leader, she resorted to that handy Celtic tradition, the geisa.

"I place a geisa on you, Dermot," said Grania. "It's death and dishonor for you unless you take me with you out of my father's house before Finn and his men wake."

Dermot had no choice but to run away with Grania into the wilderness. They had not gone many miles when Finn and his company awoke. In a rage when he realized what had been done to him, Finn ordered his men to pursue the lovers and to bring back Dermot's head.

The Fennians, however, were on Dermot's side. They could understand how a young beauty like Grania would prefer Dermot over the aging Finn, so they obediently tracked the couple down, but whenever they got too close they talked and shouted loudly to warn Dermot and Grania.

So Dermot and Grania lived in the forest, eating deer they hunted and salmon they caught, moving from camp to camp, always one step ahead of the pursuing Finn. Dermot still made an effort to respect his old chief. Every night when the couple slept, he placed a large stone between them, so that they never touched each other. When Finn and his men would find their abandoned camp and discover the stone, they knew what it meant.

Grania was fast losing patience with her handsome but reluctant sweetie. Finally, one day they crossed a river at a shallow point, and water splashed on her thigh. She turned to Dermot and remarked, "This river is bolder than you, Dermot." That remark shamed Dermot, and that night, when they went to bed, there was no stone between them. Days later, when Finn came upon that camp and found no stone, he knew what that meant, and was even more furious.

Now that the pair were truly lovers, they became a favorite of Angus, the ancient Irish god of love. Several times, when they were surrounded by Finn and his men, Angus came to their rescue by throwing over them his cloak of invisibility, which allowed them to escape. Finally, after Grania and Dermot had spent seven years in the forest, eluding the Fennians, Angus personally argued their case with Finn, who reluctantly gave in, allowed the fugitives to return to Ulster, and even gave them land, where Dermot built a huge mansion that he called Rath Grania.

But Finn never really forgave Dermot, and he plotted a sinister revenge. He waited until Grania and Dermot had two sons and were lulled into a sense of security. Then he and his men visited them at Rath Grania, and he invited Dermot to join them on a hunt for the wild boar that lived on top of the mountain, Ben Bulben. This was no ordinary wild pig, but a monstrous boar that had killed all warriors who had hunted it. Grania sensed trouble.

"Don't go, Dermot," she said. "Finn is plotting your downfall."

But, as usual in these stories, when the women sense danger, their men never listen to them. Dermot took his hound and his best spear and went with Finn.

Dermot actually managed to slay the boar, but not before it gored him dreadfully. As Dermot lay groaning in agony, Finn's chief warrior, Oscar, reminded Finn, "Only you can save Dermot, Finn Mac Cool. If he drinks water from your hands, he'll live."

Finn shrugged. "Too bad there's no water here."

"Oh yes there is, "replied Oscar. "Nine paces away from you is a spring with the sweetest water in all of Ireland."

Finn sighed, and ambled over to the spring, taking his good time. He filled his cupped hands with water, but before he reached Dermot, he let the water slip through his fingers into the ground. Oscar ordered him back to the spring, but again Finn let the water drain away before reaching the dying Dermot. This time Oscar, who like the other Fennians was on Dermot's side, growled, "I swear, old man, by the gods we worship, if you don't put water in Dermot's mouth, I'll put my spear into your body." So once more Finn went to the spring and filled his hands, but by the time he reached Dermot, the beautiful warrior was dead.

Finn rejoiced over Dermot's body. "I wish all the women of

Ireland, who find you so beautiful, could see you now, bloody and torn." He grabbed the leash of Dermot's hound, saying, "I couldn't have Dermot's woman, but I'll take his dog."

All this time, Grania had waited nervously on the ramparts of Rath Grania. When she saw Finn and his men returning without Dermot, and Finn leading Dermot's hound, she knew what that meant, and her cry of anguish could be heard all over Ireland. She and her servants climbed Ben Bulben to retrieve her lover's body, but he was gone. Angus, the god of love, had spirited his dead favorite away to his own palace in the shadowy land of the Sidhe.

Some of the legends say that the crafty Finn waited a few more years until Grania had gotten over Dermot's death, and then came courting her again, and this time she accepted him. But I think the proud, brokenhearted princess wouldn't forgive the old man who had caused her lover's death. At any rate, his own men never forgave him, and there was no longer any glory for Finn Mac Cool and his Fennians.

THE GODDESS AND THE KING

There's more than meets the eye in tales like those of Deirdre and Grania. In the very earliest Celtic civilizations, people still worshipped one all-important goddess. Only by symbolically marrying the goddess could a man be king of his tribe, just as all the men whom Queen Maeve married could only be king because they were married to her. Usually, the new king "married" the goddess by sleeping with the high priestess who symbolized her. But he didn't stay king for long. After ruling for a specified amount of time, the king was usually sacrificed, and another, younger man was made king, to rule for a while and, in his turn, be sacrificed. (Remember, Maeve had three husbands.) Both Deirdre and Grania reject an old king for a new young lover, just as the goddess did back in Ireland's prehistory. Probably, in the original stories, the two women *were* the goddess, but when their romances were recorded on paper, the Christian monks who wrote them down felt the need to add a moral. The church hardly approved of engaged women running off with cute young guys, especially without benefit of marriage! So both romances had to end tragically.

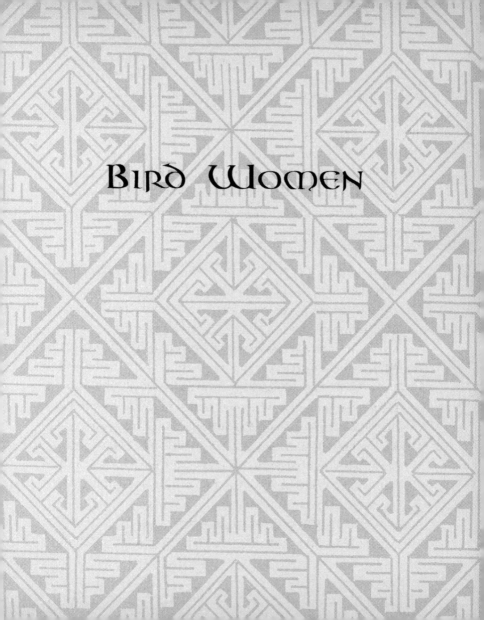

BIRD WOMEN

Caer the Swan Maiden

Ancient Irish women, both mortals and goddesses, turned themselves into birds at the drop of a hat. The Morrigan and her warrior sisters, Badb and Macha, morphed into ravens, but the birds of choice for most ancient Irish women were swans.

Caer was a maiden of the Sidhe, and Angus was the young and handsome god of love. Caer loved him from afar, but as Angus was always surrounded by beautiful Celtic groupies, as befits a god of love, he never noticed Caer. She decided to take matters into her own hands.

One night, as Angus lay in bed in his palace at Brugh Na Boyne, the fairy hill that today is called Newgrange, the most beautiful woman he had ever seen appeared to him. The love god was used to girls sneaking into his bedroom, so he reached out to pull her into his bed, but she coyly remained out of his reach. She played for him on her harp, music so sweet that it lulled him to sleep.

Of course the mysterious woman was Caer, but how could Angus know that? All he knew was that she showed up at his bedside every night for a year, putting him under the spell of her harp. By the end of the year he had grown sick from love of her. He lost all interest in the other women of the Sidhe and took to his bed, wasting away. The greatest druids of the land came to see him, but none could identify his malady. Finally a druid sent for Angus's mother, the goddess Boann. She took one look at his pale, pinched face, and understood as only a mother can.

"Why, Angus, it's sick with love you are."

"Aye, that I am, mother," he moaned, and told her the whole story.

Boann rose from her place by her son's bed. "Silly boy, to not tell me sooner. We'll have to find that girl!"

She sent runners over all of Ireland to find a woman who matched her son's description. Another year passed, and poor Angus had faded to almost nothing, when the last runner returned.

"I've found the maiden," he panted. "Her name is Caer, and she lives with her father, Ethal Anbuail, in his fairy hill in Connaught, near Loch Bel Dragon."

Angus dragged himself out of bed and mounted a chariot along with Boann and his father, the Dagda, who was king of all the Sidhe. They rode to Loch Bel Dragon and peered through the bushes. There was Caer, bathing in the river with her handmaids, and she was so tall and proud that the tallest of her maids reached only to her shoulder.

"It's her!" Angus started forward, but the Dagda grabbed his shoulder and made him wait.

"You can't run over and claim her, just like that," he said.

"There's some magic to her. We'll need help from Maeve and Ailill, the rulers of Connaught, for it's there that her home is."

So the three went to Maeve and Ailill's palace, and the royal couple were honored that the gods had paid them a visit. "What can we do for you?" asked Ailill.

When the Dagda told him, Ailill said, "We can't give you Caer, for she's a fairy woman, and we have no power over her. Maybe her father will help." And he sent a messenger to Ethal Anbuail in his fairy hill.

The messenger returned with a long face. "Ethal Anbuail won't come, and he won't help."

Maeve grinned and belted on her sword. "We'll see about that," she said. She loved a good fight!

The warrior queen led her men to Ethal Anbuail's fairy hill, and they started taking the hill apart, stone by stone. Ethal Anbuail came running out, crying, "Stop!"

Maeve's men grabbed hold of Ethal and led him to Maeve. She pointed her sword at his throat, demanding he give his daughter to Angus.

"Never," said Ethal. "I'll never wed my daughter to the son of the Dagda."

"Then prepare to lose your head," said Maeve, and she lifted her sword up in the air with both hands.

"Wait!" cried Ethal. "The truth is I *can't* give you my daughter! Caer's magic is stronger than mine."

"And what is that magic?" asked Maeve.

"Easily told. My daughter can transform herself into a swan. If Angus comes to Loch Bel Dragon this summer, he'll see 150 white swans, and that's Caer and her handmaids. The maids will be wearing silver chains, but Caer's chain will be of gold."

Maeve and Ailill let Ethal go then, and even helped restore his home. As for Angus, he could hardly wait for summer. On the first day of summer, he rode up to the enchanted lake, and watched

as 150 white swans descended on the water. Even without her golden chain, he would have recognized Caer, because she was the fairest swan of all.

He called her by name, and she turned in the water, and the feathers fell from her gleaming body. "Who calls me?" she cried.

"It's me, Angus, whose dreams you've haunted for two years. I've come to ask you to be mine."

"And about time," she muttered to herself, but she swam over to where Angus waited, rose from the water, and embraced him. As her arms surrounded him, he became a black swan. The two swans, wings clasped, encircled the lake three times before flying to Angus's home at Brugh Na Boyne. On their flight, they sang so sweetly that everyone who heard their song fell into a deep sleep for three days.

And Caer got her man by making him think *he* was getting *her*.

THE REAL SWANS OF NEWGRANGE

The tale of Angus and his swan maiden has its roots (or feathers) in reality. Every autumn, flocks of Whooper swans take off from Iceland and fly to Ireland for the winter. The flocks that arrive at Brugh Na Boyne, or Newgrange, vary from 30 birds up to as many as 226. Countless generations of swans have traced the same migratory paths in the sky for thousands of years. Were Angus and Caer the first swans to do so?

Dervorgilla

The tale of Dervorgilla, like most of the other myths in this book, was first recorded in the seventh century A.D., but all these stories date back to hundreds of years before monks first put them on parchment. I think Dervorgilla's story, which hearkens back to a time of primitive earthiness and shocking savagery, may be one of the oldest Irish stories on record. Be warned: It's not pretty.

It was not only the women of the Sidhe who could turn into birds, back in those ancient days. Mortal women, if they had some knowledge of magic, could do it, too, and most mortals knew a little magic. Dervorgilla's father was the king of Lochlinn, and he was forced to pay heavy taxes to the Fomorians, the traditional bad guys of Irish mythology. But the people of Lochlinn ran out of gold, so instead they offered up their princess. There Dervorgilla sat, chained to a rock on a deserted beach, weeping and waiting for the Fomorians to come and carry her off.

And there is where Cuchulain, on his way home from the Shadowy Isles one night, found her, killed the Fomorians, and rescued her. He was wounded in the fight, so Dervorgilla tore a strip from the hem of her dress to bind his wounds. Then she hurried home to tell her father that she was safe, and that the evil Fomorians would never bother them again.

The delighted king, who had really not wanted to lose his daughter, declared a holiday and a big feast. "Tell me who saved you," he asked his daughter, "and I'll give him your hand in marriage."

Alas, it had been too dark, and Dervorgilla never got a good look at her hero. This was all that half the men of Lochlinn had to hear. Immediately they all stepped up, claiming to be the one who had saved Dervorgilla. In the middle of the chaos, who should arrive but Cuchulain, on his way home, stopping by for the free food. Dervorgilla took one look at the bandage on his arm and recognized the cloth of her dress. It helped that Cuchulain was really, really handsome.

"This is the one, Daddy," she told her father. "Marry us right now."

Cuchulain, however, was on his way home to be married to his fiancée, Emer. Not wanting to insult the king, he simply explained that he needed to get home, and couldn't stop and marry anyone just at this moment.

"Maybe some other time," he said, as he departed in a hurry.

Dervorgilla took that to heart. Using what magic she knew, she changed herself and her maid into swans, and set out for the hero's home, to find him and marry him.

Back in Ulster, Cuchulain was out hunting with his blood brother, Lugaid, when he saw two beautiful swans, chained together with a golden chain, flying overhead. You'd think he would have decided that swans chained together with a golden chain might be some kind of magic, but not our macho Cuchulain. He fitted a stone into his slingshot and shot at the birds, wounding one. The swans fell to earth and turned into two beautiful women, one more beautiful than the other, and she wounded in her thigh. As Cuchulain ran to her side, she looked up at him in pain and disgust.

"Cuchulain, you idiot," she shouted, "don't you remember me? I'm the princess Dervorgilla, whose life you saved, coming to find you and marry you, and now look what you've done to me!"

Cuchulain felt awful. He knelt by her side, put his mouth to her thigh, and sucked the stone out from her wound. In doing so, he swallowed some of her blood, and this gave him a perfect excuse to avoid marrying her and also to avoid insulting her.

"I can't marry you, fair maiden," he said. "Because I've swallowed some of your blood, and that makes us kin. And I can't ever marry a relative."

Meanwhile Lugaid's eyes were popping. He'd never seen such a beauty, and he fell in love with her on the spot. He elbowed Cuchulain, who added, "However, if you'd like, you can marry my blood brother, Lugaid."

Dervorgilla accepted Lugaid as her husband. While he was no rock star like Cuchulain, he was pretty cute in his own way, and besides, if she married him, she would get to hang with Cuchulain.

The couple lived happily together until deepest winter. There was a heavy snow, and, as was the yearly custom, the men of Ulster built up tall pillars of snow for a unique competition that the women held: a pissing contest. The women would climb to the tops of the snow pillars and take turns peeing, to see who could melt the most snow. This wasn't just a fun, if earthy, way to pass (no pun intended) a cold winter day; these ancient women connected urine with sexual prowess, and believed that the biggest pisser was also the most sexually desirable woman. It may seem weird to us, and a little kinky too, but the ancient Irish equated bladder size with sexuality.

Dervorgilla was shy and didn't want to compete with the other women. After all, she was a stranger, and no contest like this had ever been held in her home town. But the women of Ulster insisted.

"It'll be fun, you'll see!" they cried, and dragged her to the foot of tallest snow cone.

Dervorgilla sighed, climbed to the top, squatted down, peed on the pillar of snow—and melted the whole thing down to the ground! The women of Ulster had not expected this. They started to mutter among themselves.

"This is serious," they told each other. "When our menfolk hear what Dervorgilla has done, they'll all desire her instead of us. I say we vote her off the island." They attacked the hapless princess with their knives, and mutilated her face. Dervorgilla dragged herself back to her house and prepared to die.

Meanwhile Cuchulain and Lugaid stood on a high hill overlooking their village. Suddenly they noticed that the snow on the roofs of all the houses had been melted by the fires inside, except for one—and that was the home of Lugaid and Dervorgilla. If there was no fire burning in the house on this cold winter day, something must be very wrong! The two men ran to the house and tried the door, but it was locked. Dervorgilla didn't want her husband to see her horribly maimed. As they listened through the door, she sobbed out the whole story. Then she crawled into bed and willed herself to death.

In a fury over their crime, Cuchulain pushed over all the houses of the women of Ulster. As for the heartbroken Lugaid, as he stood at Dervorgilla's grave, he died of sorrow, and was buried along with the woman he loved.

THE SWAN CHILDREN

Not all women became swans on purpose. The unfortunate children of Lir, the sea god, had no choice in the matter. Lir (whose son, Mannanan Mac Lir, was the husband of Fand) married Aebh, one of four daughters of Bodb the Red, king of the Sidhe. They had two sons and a daughter, but then Aebh died. So Lir married her sister, Aeife. But Aeife grew jealous of her stepchildren, fearing that Lir loved them more than she. She took them to Lake Darvra, and while they swam in the water, she used her magic to turn them into swans. For three hundred years they would be bound to Lake Darvra, she pronounced, then another three hundred years in the North Channel, and finally three hundred years must they spend on the Isle of Glora in Mayo, before they could return home in human form.

The grieving Lir tried to change them back, but Aeife's magic was stronger than his, so he had to content himself with punishing Aiefe by changing her into a demon of the air.

When the swan children finally returned home after nine hundred years, they found the gods had left the earth. Saint Patrick had come to Ireland, and Christianity now ruled the land. The saint himself baptized the swans into the new faith, and as soon as he poured holy water on them, they became human again.

But the years had taken their toll, and they were two ancient old men and an old woman. Soon after that, they died, and were buried all together in one grave.

Fand

You really would think that Cuchulain would stop and consider whenever he saw unusual birds, instead of automatically shooting at them. But this fabled Irish hero always seemed to be one brick short of a load. When two absolutely gorgeous birds showed up on a lake one day, linked together by a golden chain, and singing the sweetest music that anyone had ever heard, did he think that maybe there was something special about them, and that he should leave them alone? Not Cuchulain! He picked up his spear and hurled it at the birds, hitting one in the wing, whereupon both birds dived beneath the water and disappeared.

Tired after his macho spear-throwing and annoyed that he had missed, Cuchulain lay down in the sun, napping against a tall standing stone. A sound woke him, and he opened his eyes to see two women of unearthly beauty approaching him, one in a crimson cloak and one in a green cloak, each carrying a willow rod in her hand. The woman in crimson had her arm in a sling, and both women looked furious at him. They commenced beating the tar out of him with their willow rods, and the big strong hero was strangely helpless to resist.

The two women didn't stop until poor Cuchulain was half-dead. Then they disappeared, leaving him to drag his bruised body home and take to his bed. He stayed in bed, not getting any worse, but not healing either, for a year and a day, and no doctors could figure out what was wrong with him. At the end of that time, the mysterious woman in the crimson cloak appeared at his bedside. Recognizing her immediately, Cuchulain cowered beneath his covers, waiting for another attack, but she was no longer angry.

"My arm has healed, so I suppose I forgive you, Cuchulain," she told him. "But you really *are* an oaf, and you really *must* stop shooting at magical birds. My name is Liban, and I am handmaiden of Fand, wife of Mannannan Mac Lir, king of the sea. Fand and Mannannan have had a falling out, and she has set her eyes on you, and found you handsome. She invites you to come live with her in her undersea palace, and you'd have known all this a year ago, had you not shot me in the wing."

"Come live with the queen of the sea?" exclaimed Cuchulain. "You don't have to ask me twice! But look what you did to me; I can't even stand up."

"Oh, you're all better now, Cuchulain," said Liban, and she waved her hand over him. And sure enough, he was completely healed.

So Cuchulain sailed with Liban on a copper ship to the island in the middle of the water where the lovely queen of the sea, Fand, whose name means Pearl of Beauty, waited for him, surrounded by 150 handmaidens. There they slept together in a bed of gold and silver, and lived amid the most fragrant flowers and trees, and the most sweetly singing birds (and Cuchulain never took a shot at them!).

After a month, Cuchulain got homesick and wanted to go back and see his old friends and his wife. Did I mention that he had a wife? She was the long-suffering Emer, who had tolerated her husband's many flings.

"Well, if you must go home, I suppose you must, but let's meet again," suggested Fand. And they decided to meet in a week, on the seashore.

Emer lovingly welcomed Cuchulain back, until she found out that he'd spent the last month sleeping with the sea goddess and that he planned to get back together with her in a week. Long-suffering Emer was, but this was the last straw for her, and she got righteously pissed off. Without saying a word to her husband, she gathered together the women of Ulster. Armed with knives, armored with gold breastplates, they drove war chariots to the place where Cuchulain was to meet Fand, and surrounded the lovers.

Emer berated Cuchulain, "It's a wicked heartbreaker you are! Go on with your goddess, then, never mind me and my broken heart. I know the grass is always greener. And anyway, how can I compete?"

Fand was moved. "Poor girl, "she said, "I can see how much you love Cuchulain. Take him back, and I won't be standing in your way. I'll just be going back to my lonely palace beneath the waves."

"No, no," objected Emer. "It's yourself must take him. After all, you're the goddess. I'll just be going off somewhere and living out my life alone and never bother the two of you."

"No, you take him," said Fand.

"No, no, I insist. *You* take him," said Emer.

Poor Cuchulain couldn't get a word in edgewise.

Meanwhile, the women of Ulster, standing in their chariots, clutching their knives, were growing bored and wondering when they would get to fight. Finally Mannannan Mac Lir himself showed up, riding the waves on his golden chariot drawn by white horses.

"What's the problem here?" he asked. "We had a silly fight, Fand, but it's over. I'm sorry I ever criticized you for trying on all those dresses. Of course you needed to try on twenty-five gowns, to find the only one that perfectly complimented your perfect figure. Come back to me now, and leave the mortals alone."

That was all Fand needed. "Well then, I will," she declared. "After all, Cuchulain has Emer to love him, and without me, you have nobody." And, putting her dainty white hand in his, she stepped into Mannannan's chariot and sank beneath the waves. But not before Mannannan had shaken his cloak between Cuchulain and Fand, thus ensuring they would never see each other again.

He wasn't taking any chances.

FAIRY WIVES

Cuchulain wasn't the only mortal man to live with a goddess in the shadow world. Before Patrick came along to spoil the fun, goddesses liked sleeping with mortals, and there was lots of back-and-forth between worlds. Take for instance, the scary, Halloween-type tale of Nera. Nera's story begins, fittingly, on Samhain, the ancient Celtic Halloween, a dangerous time indeed, when the dead walk and fairies roam the world.

Nera was a subject of the infamous Queen Maeve and her husband, Ailill. One Samhain eve, the king and queen sat at dinner with their court. Outside, on a high hill, stood a gallows, upon which hung the corpses of two criminals. Ailill, in the spirit of the season, offered a reward to any of his men who were brave enough to touch the feet of one of the hanged men on Samhain eve.

"What's the reward?" asked Nera.

"My gold-hilted sword," replied Ailill.

That was a great reward, and greed gave Nera courage. He climbed the hill, walked up to one of the corpses and touched his foot. But on Samhain, the dead can speak, and the corpse cried out, "Water! Water!"

Nera, a brave man indeed, took pity on the dead man, lifted him off the gallows, and carried him to a nearby well, where he gave him water. Then he returned the man to the gallows, hung him neatly back up again, and started downhill to the palace. But when he got to the bottom of the hill, he found the palace in flames, and the bodies of Maeve, Ailill, and all the court, lying scattered like dry leaves on the ground.

Then Nera spied a line of armed men entering the fairy hill of Cruachan. Thinking the fairy army wouldn't notice him, he joined the line and followed them inside. But the Sidhe aren't fooled that easily, and once the men got inside, they brought him to their king. The king liked the looks of this brave mortal, so he gave him a beautiful fairy wife.

Nera couldn't believe his luck, and was happy as a clam, and his fairy wife grew to love him, too. In fact, she loved him so much that after a year was over, she decided to tell him the truth: "Your people are not really dead, and your palace was not really torched. That was a glamour that the Sidhe put on you. In fact, if you go back, you'll find that it's still Samhain, and the king and queen and all their company are still sitting at the table.

"But you must warn them that the Sidhe really do plan to attack them next Samhain, for that's the only night that we can leave our hills. Their only hope is to attack this hill first."

So Nera returned to Maeve and Ailill, who didn't even know he'd been gone, because no time had passed at all, and he repeated the

Nera's fairy wife warns him of the Sidhe's planned attack.

warning. Ailill said, "Then, if you have anything in the hill that you want to save, bring it out now, before we attack."

Nera returned to the fairy hill and brought out his wife and all his cattle, and one of those cows was the fairy cow—remember her?—that had mated with the brown bull of Cooley and had born a fairy calf. And that's how the Cattle Raid of Cooley started.

As for Nera, once the battle was over, he returned to the fairy hill with his wife, and he's still there.

PART TWO
AFTER PATRICK

Christianity arrived late to Ireland, and the church did its best to suppress gutsy women, to the point of turning their goddesses into saints. They couldn't do much with the nastier war goddesses, but Brigit, daughter of the Dagda, was a good candidate for sainthood. In fact, after they were introduced to Christianity in the fifth century, the Irish took to sainthood with such gusto, and developed so many of their own, that by the eleventh century the country became known as "the isle of saints."

In A.D. 697, a law was passed forbidding women to fight alongside their men in battle—pretty good proof for those who believed that the Irish women never *did* fight side by side with their men. However, it takes more than a little churchifying to make Irish women abandon their romantic and feisty characters. Irish women, still independent, kept their own last names after marriage. And Christianity couldn't put an end to scandalous women like Grania O'Malley, warrior queen of the seas, or Dervorgilla, Queen of Meath, who caused the ruin of Ireland by emulating her foremothers Deirdre and Grania and running off with the man she loved.

Saintly Roses and Two Sinners

Brigit: From Goddess to Saint

The first monks who arrived on the Emerald Isle's shores some time around the fifth century, hoping to convert the people, found themselves with a problem. The Irish had a wealth of song and story regarding their godlike heroes and their very human-seeming gods, and they were reluctant to give it all up for just one god. The monks' solution was to adopt some of the likelier deities, turn them into Christian saints, and turn their temples into churches.

This is what was done to Brigit, one of the most important goddesses of the ancient Irish. In some legends, Brigit was the daughter of the Dagda, king of the Tuatha De Danaan. In others, she was equated with Danu herself, the great mother goddess of the Sidhe. Her name meant Fiery Arrow, and she was definitely a fire goddess. Stories tell that a column of fire rose from her head. She had a shrine at Kildare, where nineteen virgins tended her sacred fire, which never went out. But she was also the goddess of poetry and of healing.

Saint Brigit inherited all the goddess's traits. It was said that she, too, had a column of fire rising from her head, and that when she was a baby, the house she slept in appeared to be on fire, but she was never burned. After the advent of Christianity, the goddess's sacred fire continued to be tended by virgins, but now the virgins were nuns.

According to her church-approved story, Saint Brigit was born in 453, of a Christian mother, Brocessa, and a nobleman named Dubthatch. Brocessa was Dubthatch's slave, and his jealous wife made him sell Brocessa to a druid. This Dubthatch did, but with the stipulation that the unborn baby was his, and would be returned to him when it was old enough. Growing up in a druid's household was a handy thing for a future saint; Brigit would

learn a thing or two about religion, and, if she was smart, get some ideas of her own, which seems to be what happened.

Little Brigit went to work in the druid's dairy, but she gave away as much butter and milk to the poor as the cows produced. When the druid heard she was giving away his butter, he marched angrily down to the dairy and demanded she show him a full tub of butter—or else. There was only half a tub of butter left, because Brigit had been giving away butter like there was no tomorrow, but miraculously, the tub kept refilling itself, so the druid had all the butter he wanted. Being a druid, he understood that this was no ordinary little girl, so he fell to his knees before her, and offered to give her his cows.

"I don't want your cows," said little Brigit. "Just free my mother."

So Brigit earned her mother's freedom.

When she was eleven or twelve, Brigit's father sent for her, and she went to live with Dubthatch, his wife, and her stepbrothers. Immediately, she was up to her old tricks, giving away all the family's wealth to the poor. Finally Dubthatch had had it up to there with his charitable little brat, and he loaded her into his cart, to sell her to the high king.

He parked his cart outside the palace gates and left Brigit in it. In those days, you didn't enter into a king's presence with your sword buckled on, so he left his sword, too. No doubt you can guess what happened next, and you're right. A leper came by, begging for charity, and Brigit gave him her father's sword.

When Dubthatch came for his daughter and discovered she'd given away his sword, he was, as you can imagine, at wit's end. He dragged the girl into the throne room, and threw her down in front of the king.

"Take my wretched daughter!" he bellowed. "If she stays in my house one more week, she'll reduce us to beggars!"

The king thought, And if I take her, soon it'll be my wealth she gives away. Besides, it so happened that he had just been baptized into that new Christian religion. So he ordered Dubthatch to take Brigit home, but also to keep a careful eye on his treasury.

Brigit grew into a beautiful young woman, and her family was after her to marry. She had her choice of eager suitors, too, but of course she'd promised herself to Jesus. When her father and brothers became too insistent, she mutilated her own face, so that no one would want her. At this, long-suffering Dubthatch gave up.

"Okay," he told her. "If you want to be a nun so badly, go be a nun."

And he gave her money and a ship. With her seven girlfriends, who were as zealous about this newfangled Christianity as she was, Brigit traveled to Croghan Hill, where the girls were baptized and ordained by Saint Mel. As soon as she was ordained as a nun, Brigit's beauty miraculously returned. She then went on to found the first convent in Ireland, in Kildare.

How she got the land for her convent involves another miracle. She asked the king of Leinster for as much land as her mantle would cover, but when she threw the mantle on the ground, it spread and spread until it seemed it might cover all of Ireland. Hastily, the king snatched it off the ground and gave her the land.

Did I mention that the goddess Brigit also had a miraculous mantle?

The similarities continue: Brigit was goddess of healing; Saint Brigit was forever miraculously healing hopelessly sick people. And of course there are those crosses made from rushes that can be found all over Ireland even today. Their design is ancient, and they are called Brigit's crosses, but whether Brigit is the ancient goddess or the later saint doesn't seem to matter. Good luck is good luck.

BRIGIT, TIME TRAVELER?

The most popular legend surrounding Saint Brigit would require her to have the time-traveling abilities of Xena, warrior princess, who somehow managed to encounter every historical character from Gilgamesh to Julius Caesar during the life of her television series.

One of Brigit's many names is "foster mother of Christ." According to legend, she either served as midwife to Mary for Jesus' birth, wrapped the infant Jesus in that miraculous mantle of hers, baby-sat for the little darling while Mary napped, or—most intriguing of all, happened to be at the scene when King Herod's soldiers, searching for the Holy Family, almost caught up with them. By balancing an elaborate candelabra on her head, she managed to distract the soldiers long enough for Jesus, Mary, and Joseph to escape.

How Brigit, supposedly born in Ireland in the fifth century, could have wound up in Bethlehem in time for the birth of Christ, we leave up to the church for explanation.

The Countess Kathleen O'Shea

The church never tried to canonize the Countess Kathleen O'Shea, so she remains a charming Irish legend, demonstrating that it's perfectly permissible to do wrong for the right cause, and even get rewarded while you're at it.

The saintly (and as usual, beauteous) countess lived long ago, shortly after Saint Patrick had brought Christianity to Ireland, and she was one of its most pious practitioners. Her tenants, farmers, and townspeople all followed the new Christian religion and had put the old gods behind them. Crops grew and were harvested, hens laid eggs, bees made honey, and cows gave milk. Life was good.

Until one year it all ended. There was no rain that year, none at all. With no water, the crops withered and died in the ground. With no flowers to pollinate, the bees shrugged their wings and went away. With no grass to eat, the cows' milk dried up, and with no grain to peck, the hens laid no eggs. The milkless cows and eggless chickens were slaughtered for food, because the people had to eat something, and they hopefully sowed a new crop for the next year and prayed at the church for rain.

But no rains came. Next summer the countess's subjects ate up all their seed corn. She gave away her own stored wheat to the people, and then that was gone too. Soon her subjects were reduced to eating the wild grasses of the forest, and they didn't live long on that. Wakes and burials became a common thing.

Of course, there were those misers who had held onto their cattle and kept their grain stores, so they had food to sell to the hungry, but being greedy, they demanded prices that none could pay, at least not after they had sold all their furniture and worldly goods, and mortgaged their houses.

Countess Kathleen sent for all her riches; her golden crowns, necklaces, ruby rings, and gold and silver coins. She divided her wealth in half, giving each half to a trusted servant. The only gold she kept for herself was the gold of her hair, and the only rubies left were the red of her lips.

"Take this," she told one servant. "Buy a ship and sail to England. In England, buy all the grain the ship will hold, and bring it back here for my people."

And, "Take this," she told the other servant. "Take my swiftest horse and ride to the other end of Ireland, where it still rains. Buy all the cattle you can, and drive them back here for my people."

Then she went to church, and prayed for a safe voyage and fast return.

Meanwhile, two strangers arrived at her village and found lodging at the local inn. Well fleshed and dressed in velvets and furs, the newcomers stood out among the haggard, ragged scare-crows of the village. They were handsome men, with flashing eyes and curling hair, and with white, slightly pointed teeth. What did they want here, the villagers wondered. "We're traders," said the strangers, showing off leather pouches stuffed with gold, "work-ing for a powerful master, and we're paying good prices."

But for what? "We've nothing left to trade for," said the vil-lagers. "No crops, no cattle, just us living skeletons, and soon we won't even be living anymore."

"Ah, but you do have something we want, and that we're will-ing to pay for," answered the strange men, and they smiled wide smiles with pointy white teeth. "We'll pay good money for your souls, every one of you."

These were good, pious people, but they were also *starving* people. Soon one after another showed up trembling and fright-ened at the inn, signed a very special parchment with their blood, and danced out of the inn laughing and tossing around their new golden treasure. With no souls to trouble them, they no longer cared about being good to one another. Wife left husband and husband ran off with someone else's wife. Children were aban-doned while the soulless villagers drank and caroused and fought with eachother.

Breezes carried noise from the streets up to the parapet of Kathleen's castle, where she waited day after day, watching for the tall mast of the ship full of grain, or for the dust in the distance that must mean a great herd of cattle was arriving. She didn't realize how long it takes for a herd of cattle to travel the length of Ireland, and she didn't know that her ship sat becalmed in mid-ocean, waiting for a wind to fill its sails.

Finally, she couldn't ignore the sounds of screaming, shouting, and mad laughter coming from below. "What *is* going on down there?" she asked a servant. "That doesn't sound like starving people."

"The people aren't starving anymore, your grace," answered a flustered servant, "or rather, they've left their babies to starve while they riot and drink, because they don't care anymore. Their souls are gone, sold to the devil."

Kathleen hadn't realized that it had come to this. She took one long look back, but there was still no ship, no cattle to be seen. She descended the stone castle stairs on her dainty satin-slippered feet, and entered the church. She knelt at the altar and prayed, for a long time. The sun fell and the moon rose and still she prayed. Finally, as the sun rose again, red in the sky, she stood, gathered up her long velvet skirts and proceeded to the inn.

The two handsome strangers had been waiting for her. One held the door open, while the other bowed low from his waist.

"At last, Countess," he said. "You honor us with your visit."

Kathleen looked at them coldly, and they smiled back with their white, pointy teeth. "You know why I am here?"

"Oh yes," they breathed, and one of them steered her to a polished mahogany desk, while the other held out an elegantly carved chair for her. One held out a parchment with strange writing on it, writing that seemed to writhe all over the page. The other offered her a tiny silver pen knife, to cut her finger with.

"If you'll just sign here," they murmured.

"Not so fast," said the countess. "My price is high."

"Of course, of course," they sighed. "For someone like you, anything."

Kathleen did some quick addition in her head. "I must have 50,000 gold coins," she began. That, she thought, would buy enough food for her subjects, even from the greediest merchants, until the wheat and cattle arrived.

"Oh, done, done!" The two traders rubbed their hands together, but the countess continued.

"And you must return the souls of all my people."

"Easily done, easily done. Our master didn't really want their silly dried-up souls anyway. It was your soul he sent us for, sweet and rich as Devonshire cream."

Kathleen took the offered pen knife, pricked her finger without flinching, and signed the parchment.

Kathleen signs away her soul.

In the wink of an eye, all the villagers got their souls back. The bottles fell from their hands as they realized what they had been doing. The strayed husbands ran back to their wives, and the mothers ran quickly home, where their babies lay hungry and crying. But everyone stopped in mid-run when they saw Countess Kathleen O'Shea stagger out the door of the inn, the gold in her hair tarnished now and dull, falling over her lowered face, the skirt of her velvet gown dragging in the dust. Silently they lined up on either side of her as she passed them, knowing what she had done for them, not daring to speak, but one young girl kissed the dusty hem of her dress as she walked by.

Kathleen went straight to her room, changed into a long linen nightgown and took to her bed, not speaking or eating. By morning she was dead.

This was when a curious thing happened. Kathleen's old nurse, praying and weeping by the bedside of her dead mistress, heard the music of a harp, and looked up. Lighting the dim room with their radiance, sixteen angels hovered over the countess's bed, and as the nurse watched, Kathleen's glowing soul—taken back from the devil—rose from her still body and accompanied the angels, through the ceiling, through the roof of the castle, and up to heaven.

The rains came back that winter, but before that, the cattle and wheat bought by Countess Kathleen arrived in time to keep her people from starvation. As for the traders, with their curling hair and white, pointy teeth, it's said that they're still in hiding from the devil, who doesn't like to be tricked.

119 IRISH SAINTS

The early Irish church, as far as sainthood went, was pretty much an equal opportunity employer, and an ancient Latin text, the *Martyrology of Tallaght,* listed some 119 female Irish saints.

Next to Brigit, Ireland's most important female saint was Saint Ita, who was known as the Brigit of Munster. Ita was, as usual, a beautiful princess, but when her father tried to marry her off to a neighboring chieftain, she refused, insisting that she wished to be a nun. Unlike Brigit, she didn't have to mutilate herself to keep her virginity; instead, her father received a heaven-sent vision and let her have her way. She journeyed to western Limerick and there founded a convent and a school, where she educated so many future saints that she became known as "the mother of saints."

A true mother of saints was Saint Patrick's sister, Saint Darerca. She was married twice, and by both husbands she had a total of sixteen sons and two daughters, all of whom became saints when they grew up. So you didn't have to be a virgin to be a saint. In fact,

Saint Dymphna.

Saint Edith of Polesworth, daughter of King Edward the Elder of England, became an Irish saint by virtue of her marriage to the king of Dublin.

My favorite Irish saint, by dint of both her pathetic story and her fabulous name, is Saint Dymphna. Like her saintly sisters, she was the Christian daughter of a pagan chieftain, but her father was worse than any of the others. At the age of fifteen, she had to run away from home when he tried to have an incestuous relationship with her. Christian lore attempts to soften the story by pointing out that he'd been driven mad by the death of his wife, but incest is incest. Along with her old priest, Saint Gereburnus, and two religious girl-friends, she fled to Belgium, where the refugees built a small church and lived like hermits until her mad father caught up with them. He had her friends killed and beheaded her himself.

Because of her crazed father, Saint Dymphna is the patron saint of the mentally ill, but more important, she's also the patron saint of incest survivors and runaways.

Dervorgilla, Princess of Meath

The Irish sure do love to fight, and they spent most of the twelfth century doing nothing but that. All the petty kings took turns invading each other's kingdoms, and some of them even got on the wrong side of Ireland's high king, Rory O'Connor. One of these was Malachy, king of Meath, who decided that the safest way to protect himself against being invaded by the high king was to ally himself to the strong warrior chieftain, Tiernan O'Rourke. This he proceeded to do by marrying off his daughter, the princess Dervorgilla, to O'Rourke.

It's doubtful that Dervorgilla had any say in the matter. O'Rourke was not the handsomest of men; in fact, his nickname was Monoculus, meaning "one eye." Besides which, Dervorgilla already had a lover, Dermot MacMurrough, king of Leinster.

To make matters worse, when High King Rory O'Connor finally *did* invade Meath, O'Rourke did nothing, declaring himself neutral. Perhaps he was a little less than neutral, because after the war, Rory O'Connor made O'Rourke the new king of Meath, so he must have done *something* to deserve that honor.

None of these actions, of course, served to make Dervorgilla love her husband any better, so she sent out word by way of her brother, that should her old lover Dermot show up and carry her away, she probably wouldn't object very much. Dermot already had good reason to hate O'Rourke—during an earlier battle, O'Rourke had broken one of the sacred laws of medieval Ireland by slaughtering all the cows of Leinster—so this was all he needed to hear.

Taking advantage of O'Rourke's absence on a pilgrimage, Dermot invaded his castle and staged an "abduction," complete with a struggling, screaming Dervorgilla, who nevertheless made sure to bring along all her cattle, furniture, and treasures.

The lovers managed to stay together for two years before High king Rory O'Connor, taking Dermot's son and nephew hostage, forced the king of Leinster to return an unwilling Dervorgilla to her O'Rourke. In some versions of this history, Dervorgilla was then banished to a convent, but others say that Dervorgilla had no intention of staying with her hated, if legal, husband anyway, and went back home to live with her deposed father, ex-king Malachy.

Whichever his wife's actions, they didn't put O'Rourke in a forgiving mood, and he finally succeeded in getting Dermot banished from Ireland and seizing Leinster for himself. Dermot was not the kind of man to go quietly. He sailed for England, where he obtained an audience with King Henry II, inviting the king to return with him and invade Ireland. King Henry, busily invading other countries at the moment, nevertheless wrote Dermot a letter

that enabled him to enlist the support of a Norman general called Strongbow. (All of this happened after 1066, the year of the Norman invasion of England, so these "English" people were actually Normans.)

Dermot, Strongbow, and an army of 1,200 soldiers invaded Ireland and restored Dermot to the throne of Leinster. Then they descended on the high king himself. But Rory O'Connor still held Dermot's son and nephew as hostages, and he had them killed, and their bodies delivered to Dermot trussed up in a sack like slaughtered animals.

This action took the will to live out of Dermot. He disbanded his army, returned to his castle, and died there a few months later. O'Rourke didn't outlive him by much. He was beheaded by a Norman leader, Hugo deLacy, and his head was impaled on the city gate of Dublin.

Dervorgilla survived them both by twenty-one years, reached the venerable age of eighty-five, and had a beautiful nun's chapel built at the convent of Clonmacnoise, where she died in 1193.

As for the English, they simply stayed on. For this reason, to this day the Irish hold Dervorgilla personally responsible for Ireland remaining under English rule until the War of Independence freed Southern Ireland in 1922. And the British still haven't left Northern Ireland. All this resulted from two short years of unbridled passion!

THOSE DARN ROYAL MARRIAGES!

When will they ever learn? From the time of Deirdre and Naoise, Grania and Dermot, and Dervorgilla and *her* Dermot, the unwilling brides and fiancées of kings always seem to love, and to run away with, other guys. It never ends happily! The Irish princess, fair Iseult, was promised to King Mark of Cornwall, but fell in love with his nephew, Tristan, instead. To complicate matters, there was another Iseult, called Iseult of the White Hands, living in Brittany, and she too was in love with Tristan. You won't be surprised to learn that their love triangle ended tragically, with everyone involved dying of broken hearts.

This royal nonsense still goes on today, though with a sex change. Poor Charles loved Camilla but couldn't marry her. Instead, he had to marry a "proper" bride, Diana. And we all know how that turned out!

Biddy Early, the Witch of Clare

Only the church considered Biddy Early a sinner. To her neighbors for miles around, she was the Wise Woman of Clare, and her little thatched cottage was always crowded with people seeking her advice and her miraculous cures. Listed among those who came to Biddy for help were the queen of the gypsies and the Prince of Wales. In the tradition of all wise women, Biddy took no money for her cures and predictions, but if you wanted to bring her anything from a whole pig to a jug of good whiskey, so much the better, and in her house there was always a drop of drink to be shared with those who came thirsty off the road.

Bridget Ellen Connors Early was born in 1798, the daughter of John Thomas Connors and Ellen Early. Like her mother, who had some reputation as a healer, she kept her maiden name, despite having, like Queen Maeve, four husbands (all of whom died of drink). But Biddy was no warrior queen; in an earlier time she might have been a druidess, or perhaps a devotee of her namesake, Brigit, the goddess of healing. In her own time she was a *cailleach*, the wise old woman aspect of those ancient goddesses who used to change from beautiful young woman to crone and back again in the blink of an eye. Like all Irish women who are

touched by magic, she was described as having blazing red hair, and she wore a gold ring on every finger.

The source of Biddy's power lay in a small dark blue bottle, in which she could see the past, present, and future. It was widely believed that Biddy acquired her vast knowledge of healing herbs during the seven years she lived with the fairies, and she boasted that along with speaking English and Irish, she knew the language of the Sidhe. But it's likely that as a child she learned all about herbs and potions from her mother.

Stories abounded of how she got the bottle. Some said that her son, Tom, who died young, returned from the grave to give her a gift of it; others that he won it from the Sidhe, playing at the Irish game of hurling. My favorite version is that as a teenager, Biddy was baby-sitting a neighbor's child when the fairies stole the baby away and left a changeling in its place. The changeling, a child of the Sidhe, grew so fond of Biddy that he gave her the bottle.

People came to Biddy for help when they or a loved one were sick, or when they believed the fairies had cursed their sheep or cattle. She would consult her magic bottle, and if she saw a coffin in it, she would send the people away, for there was nothing to be done. Otherwise, she would send them off with a potion in a little bottle, and instructions to carry the bottle carefully and not spill it; many a sad story ended with the bottle dropped or broken on the way home, and the cure lost.

In the late nineteenth and early twentieth centuries, when the folklorist Lady Gregory traveled the countryside, collecting stories from farmers and villagers, many people she spoke with still remembered Biddy and had their own tales of miraculous cures. It was these cures that made the priests rant against her in their sermons, and in the words of one Daniel O'Shea, as taken down by Lady Gregory, "It was all you could do to get to Biddy Early with your skin whole, the priests were so set against her."

Another man, simply described by Lady Gregory as "an old man from Kinvara," took a paralyzed friend to see Biddy in hopes of a cure, and said, "I had to work to get him a lodging that night . . . for the priests had all the people warned against letting anyone in that had been to her." Once a priest rode over to Biddy's cottage in an attempt to put a stop to her goings on, and Biddy put a spell on his horse so that it stopped in the middle of the road and couldn't be made to go any further. The poor priest had to follow Biddy's instructions, which were to spit on the horse and say, "God bless you," before the horse would budge.

Eventually, in 1865, Biddy was put on trial for witchcraft, but the charges were dismissed when her accusers could find nobody to testify against her. Three years later, she married her last husband, a man half her age who came to her for a cure. Biddy must have liked what she saw, for she said that she'd cure him only on condition that he marry her, which is what he did. Twice his age or not, she outlived him anyway, as she had all her husbands.

Toward the end of her life, she was described by Lady Gregory's old man from Kinvara as "all shaky, and the crankiest woman I ever saw." When Biddy finally died in 1874, it was with a priest at her bedside and a rosary around her neck, for she was taking no chances. Twenty-seven more priests came to her funeral, so maybe they thought she wasn't such a sinner after all.

In the 1960s there was an attempt made to restore Biddy Early's cottage, perhaps to turn it into a quaint Ye Olde Tea House for tourists, but everything went wrong. Workers got sick, equipment broke down. The Sidhe had decided that a Biddy Early pub and a Biddy Early brewery were enough; they wanted their old friend's house left alone. Work on the cottage stopped, and today it stands a crumbling, roofless ruin. Visitors leave coins and crystals on the windowsills, tributes to Ireland's last great witch.

As for the magic bottle, Biddy entrusted it to the priest at her deathbed, and he threw it into Kilbarron Lake, where it still lies.

THE WITCHES OF IRELAND

Although the Irish Catholic Church was hardly fond of witches, Ireland never shared in Europe's witch-burning mania. Perhaps this was because so many of their congregation continued to practice the old ways. They dutifully went to church on Sunday, and then put out saucers of milk for the wee folk on Monday. The church would have had to throw most of the countryside into prison! Most historians believe that from the fourteenth century until people finally stopped such nonsense, only about four women were ever burned for witchcraft in Ireland.

A certain Dame Alice Kyteler, who never *was* burned, was one of the most notorious witches in the history of witchcraft. Unlike Biddy Early, Alice Kyteler was in no way a good witch or anything remotely resembling a wise woman. Perhaps she wasn't even a real witch, but merely a particularly nasty person, and definitely a poisoner.

Born in 1280 to a banker father, who built Kyteler's Inn in Kilkenny in 1300, she inherited Daddy's fortune and his inn when he died. Then she went on a marrying spree, wedding four husbands in a period of twenty years. Like Biddy Early, she outlived them all, but unlike Biddy's husbands, these guys did not die natural deaths. They were all bankers or successful businessmen, and as Alice inherited each husband's property, she grew richer and became the most important woman in Kilkenny.

The bubble burst when her last hubby, John Le Poer, acquired a mysterious wasting sickness. Grown feeble as an old man, his hair and fingernails falling out, he suspected his wife was slowly poisoning him, and went to the friars at Saint Francis's Abbey with accusations of witchcraft. He died anyway, but the friars sent for the bishop of Ossory, who dug up enough juicy evidence to prosecute Alice. Among his accusations: Alice led a coven of witches, who were in the habit of cooking up a demonical stew consisting of the fingernails of corpses, the hair and brains of unbaptized babies, worms, and chicken guts, all stirred together in a pot made from the skull of a beheaded thief. After their nightly banquets, the coven would blow out their candles (made from human fat) and cry, "Fi! Fi! Fi! Amen."

Alice also developed a novel way to ensure that her son from her first marriage, William Outlawe, had enough pocket money. In the wee morning hours, while Kilkenny still slept, she would sneak out with her broom, and sweep all the town's trash toward William's door, murmuring:

To the house of William my sonne

Hie all the wealth of Kilkennie towne.

Unfortunately for the bishop, Dame Alice had friends in high places, and it was the bishop who got arrested instead of Alice.

He spent seventeen days in the dungeons before he straightened things out, got himself freed, and finally put Alice and her coven behind bars. Only one of them, Petronilla of Meath, confessed to witchcraft, probably to avoid further torture, and she and Alice were condemned to death. Poor Petronilla was burned at the stake, but Dame Alice escaped to England, where she apparently lived out the rest of her life in peace and died of old age.

Two Pirate Queens and a Drama Queen

Grania O'Malley

There was something about Connaught that seemed to produce warrior women. The very real and historical Grania O'Malley, pirate queen of Connaught, was a likely successor to the mythical Maeve, warrior queen of Connaught. Maybe it was the water.

Born in 1530, Grania was the daughter of Owen "Black Oak" O'Malley, a chieftain of County Mayo, a seafaring man and a pirate himself, who owned a small fleet of ships. The family motto was *Terra Marique Potens:* powerful by land and sea. Of course, girls weren't supposed to go to sea like the menfolk, but young Grania wasn't content to stay home in the drafty family castle and learn women's work. She cut off her hair and dressed in boys' clothing, hoping her father might relent and take her along on his voyages if she looked like a boy. This earned her the nickname Grania Mhoal, or Grania of the Cropped Hair, a name that stuck with her for life.

Apparently it did the trick, because Grania learned sailing on her father's ship. Good thing, too, because as a result she saved his life. Their ship was under attack, and Owen had sent his daughter safely below decks, where he no doubt believed girls belonged during a battle. Grania, being Grania, disobeyed and hid herself in the rigging. When she saw an attacker coming up on her father from behind, she hurled herself onto his back like a howling, kicking, biting little monkey.

At the age of sixteen, Grania was married off to Donal O'Flaherty, son of a Connemara chieftain, and she moved into his castle on the coast of Bunowen, from which they had nice access to all the passing ships they wanted to raid. Donal, like his family and like Grania's father, was a pirate, and his young wife gladly joined him in that endeavor. They had a good little protection racket going: passing ships gladly paid to avoid being plundered. When he wasn't robbing ships, Donal, who had a fiery temper, was fighting his neighbors.

As in the days of Dervorgilla, everyone in Ireland was still fighting everyone else, with the addition of the British, who, having come over in the twelfth century, had never left and were a thorn in the side of the feuding chieftains. Around the time that Grania and Donal married, the British king Henry VIII pressured the Irish chieftains to submit to his rule. Needless to say, the O'Malleys and O'Flahertys were chief among those who resisted.

Eventually Donal's fighting ways proved the end of him, and he was killed by his traditional enemies, the Joyce clan, who then proceeded to attack the couple's castle. Grania successfully defended her castle, but the laws of the day prohibited her from inheriting

it, and she had to return home to Daddy, with her three children in tow.

After the death of her father, Grania took over his ships and his men. Even though she could not legally be made a chieftain, she acted like one and was treated like one. She moved into a castle on Clare Island, a small, underpopulated island on Clew Bay, where she had access to the rich merchant ships that sailed by, ripe for the plucking. Soon she commanded two hundred men, three galleys, and several smaller ships, and continued her plunder. Along the way she got herself a lover, who was then murdered by a neighboring clan, the MacMahons. In revenge, Grania attacked the MacMahon ships and their castle, and killed the man responsible for her lover's death.

Grania also acquired legendary status. People spoke of how, when her castle was attacked by the British, she melted down the lead roof and poured the molten lead onto the heads of her attackers. Another story told how she taught manners to the lord of Howth Castle. On her way back from Dublin, Grania stopped to rest at Howth Castle, where she expected to be treated with the hospitality that was due to her as a chieftain. Instead, the lord of the castle shut his gates to her and sent word for her to scat. Scat she did, taking with her the lord's son, whom she met on the way out, and holding him hostage. For the boy's ransom, she demanded that the lord never again shut his gate to strangers, and that he always keep a place set at the table for anyone who might need it—a custom that continues to this day.

Somewhere along the way, Grania also had another baby, either by her lover or by her second husband, "Iron Richard" Burke, whom she married in 1567. The boy was named Tibbot Ne Long, or Toby of the Ships, because she gave birth to him on board her ship.

By the time of her marriage to Iron Richard, who—guess what?—was a pirate, Grania had grown strong enough to have the upper hand. Still smarting from having lost everything after her Donal's death, she made Richard promise that if the two split up, she'd get back her dowry of cattle and horses. Their marriage was a stormy one, with Grania often threatening to divorce Richard, and at least once she locked him out of his own castle. Nevertheless the couple stayed together until Richard's death.

When the British deputy, Sir Henry Sydney, met the couple in 1576, he immediately saw who was the stronger of the two, and wrote, "a most famous feminine sea-captain called Grania O'Malley . . . offered her services to me wherever I would command her, with three galleys and 200 fighting men, either in Ireland or in Scotland. She brought with her husband, for she was, as well by sea as by land, more than master's mate to him." Sir Henry made Richard a knight, and Grania became Lady Burke, although she never seems to have called herself by that name.

Meanwhile, Grania and Iron Richard were being harassed by Sir Richard Bingham, the British governor of Connaught. He was her nemesis, her Inspector Javert, her pit bull. He described her as the "nurse of all rebellions in Connaught for the last forty years," and wasn't about to rest until he saw her behind bars. And he did arrest her twice—the first time in 1577. The Lord Justice Drury described her as "a woman that hath impudently passed the part of womanhood and had been a great spoiler and chief commander and director of thieves and murderers at sea," and had her imprisoned in Dublin castle for two years. She got out of that predicament on her own, but was captured again by Bingham in 1586, and this time he intended to hang her. He quickly built a gallows with Grania's name on it, but her son-in-law saved her by taking her place as a hostage.

With her son-in-law in prison, Grania was free, but insecure. There was only one thing to do. She went over Bingham's head, to Queen Elizabeth herself. In August 1593, Grania sailed to London, asked for and was granted an interview with the queen.

It must have been quite a meeting. Both were tough old broads in their sixties, and if Elizabeth was queen of England, well, Grania was the world's most famous pirate queen. By all accounts, they got along smashingly. Elizabeth presented Grania with a lap dog and embroidered handkerchiefs. More important, she also presented the pirate queen with a letter granting her full pardon and a pension, and ordering Bingham to leave her alone and to release her son-in-law.

Bingham was arrested on unrelated charges two years later, and Grania was finally free to plunder the high seas once more. By this time she was a bit long in the tooth for a pirate's life, so she stayed home and let her men do the hard work.

She died peacefully in bed in 1603, the same year as did her old friend, Queen Elizabeth.

ANOTHER CELTIC PIRATE QUEEN

Even before Grania O'Malley ruled the seas, another Celtic woman pirate fought for her country's independence and struck terror into the hearts of would-be conquerors. In this case, the conquered country was Celtic Brittany, then known as Armorica, and the conquerors were the French.

During the fourteenth century, a twenty-year-long war raged in Brittany, as France tried to annex the country. When a patriotic Breton nobleman, Olivier de Clisson, was executed by orders of the French king, Olivier's wife, Jeanne de Clisson, vowed revenge. Selling all her possessions, she bought three black ships and outfitted them with red sails. Jeanne became a pirate queen known as the Lioness of Brittany. Between 1343 and 1360, she was the terror of the Normandy coast, destroying French ships and torching entire villages.

Jeanne's maiden name was Jeanne de Belleville, and some sources list Jeanne de Belleville and Jeanne de Clisson as two different women, thus making it sound like there were *two* Breton pirate queens ruling the English Channel between 1343 and 1360—and that they were both named Jeanne.

To add to the confusion, during this period two noblemen, Jean de Montfort, representing Celtic Brittany, and Charles de

Blois, representing France, were duking it out (no pun intended) over who would become Duke of Brittany. Charles captured Jean in 1343 and threw him into the dungeons, whereupon Jean's wife, Jeanne de Montfort, also known as "the Flame," dressed in full armor, defended their castle against the French, and joined with the British to fight against France. Quite a coincidence! Jeanne de la Flamme, as she was called, sometimes gets confused with Jeanne the pirate queen—a case of too many Jeannes.

Anne Bonny

Ask most people about women pirates and they'll say "Anne Bonny." In fact, most people don't even know that there were any other women pirates. And they don't know that the red-haired queen of the Spanish Main was Irish.

Born Anne Cormac in County Cork in 1700, Anne was the daughter of a married lawyer, William Cormac, and his housemaid. When Cormac's wife discovered the affair, she left him, and he and his lover lived together with little Anne, but scandalized clients soon deserted him, and his business failed. When Anne was about six years old, the three split for Charleston, South Carolina, where Dad bought a plantation and resumed his law practice. Young Anne grew up rich, spoiled, and impetuous, as good as the boys with guns and horses. She had a fiery temper to match her hair, and is reported to have once knifed a servant girl in the stomach in a fit of pique. She also beat up a boy who had the nerve to make a pass at her, and put him in the hospital.

At the age of sixteen, Anne met and married a sometime-sailor, sometime-pirate name of Jim Bonny, and her indignant father promptly disinherited her. "Who cares," sniffed Anne, and the couple headed for New Providence, an island in the Bahamas that was crawling with pirates, but not before burning down Daddy's plantation.

Anne quickly tired of Bonny, who had become a snitch for Captain Woods Rogers, soon to be governor of Nassau. That's when she met the dashing pirate, "Calico Jack" Rackham, who is credited with having designed the famous skull-and-crossbones pirate flag, the Jolly Roger. The couple fell hard for each other, and Calico Jack offered to buy Anne from her husband.

The governor got wind of this disgraceful behavior and threw the two in prison, vowing to have Anne whipped and returned to her rightful husband. Instead, Anne and Jack, out on bail, rounded up a crew of eight pirate buddies, stole a sloop, and made off for the high seas. Anne took to the pirate's life like a duck takes to water, dressing in men's clothing and becoming an expert with pistols, machetes, and rapiers, and often leading the men when they boarded a captured ship.

No story of Anne Bonny can be told without including Mary Read. Unlike Anne, Mary had spent most of her life in male attire. Her mother pretended the child was a boy in order to get an inheritance from her mother-in-law. She'd had a baby boy who had died, and in those days, girls couldn't inherit. So she dressed daughter Mary up in her dead brother's clothing and passed her off as "Mark," probably the brother's name. At the age of thirteen, Mary was hired by a rich French lady to serve

"Lady of the Black Flag," from a 1947 comic book.

as footboy. That job didn't last long because Mary craved adventure, and she found it by joining the army, still, of course, disguised as a boy. It was in the army that she met and fell in love with a fellow soldier. She revealed her true sex, left the army, and married him. The two opened an inn, and for a brief time Mary actually dressed in women's clothing, but her husband died young, and it was back to men's attire and to a life on the open seas for Mary.

This was when Anne met Mary. Stories differ; some say Calico Jack had known and sailed with Mary before, some say he was completely clueless about her true sex. At any rate, first Anne, then Jack, learned the truth about Mary, and she joined them in their pirating adventures. The two women, the only women pirates of the Caribbean, became fast friends. There's a theory that they were lesbian lovers. What is more likely is that, with their apparently devil-may-care attitude of "anything goes," they were bisexual. Certainly Anne had Jack, and Mary had a boyfriend over whom she once fought a duel.

In August 1720, a pirate hunter named Capt. James Barnet attacked Calico Jack's sloop, the *William*, and fired on it. Rackham and most of the men, drunk as skunks, took refuge from the cannonballs below decks, but Anne and Mary, with a few of the braver men, stayed on deck, fighting back. Later, in court, Barnet would testify that the two women fought fiercely with pistols, cutlasses, and axes. Furious at the crew's cowardice, Anne screamed down to them, "If there's a man among ye, ye'll come out and fight like the men ye are!" Then she and Mary emptied their guns into the hold, killing one of their own men and wounding two others, including Calico Jack.

Finally the pirates surrendered and were brought to trial in Jamaica. The men were tried first, found guilty, and hanged. Anne was permitted to see Calico Jack before his execution, but if he expected tearful sympathy, he was mistaken. Regarding him with scorn, she said, "I'm sorry to see you like this, Jack. But if you had fought like a man, you need not have been hang'd like a dog."

Twelve days later the women came to trial. The judge had just pronounced the expected sentence upon them—that they be hanged by the neck—when Anne and Mary spoke up: "Milord, we plead our bellies."

They were pregnant! Under the law, a pregnant woman could not be executed, because that meant taking the life of an innocent unborn baby. Instead, the woman was sent back to her cell until her baby was born, and *then* she was killed. The poor baby was sent to an orphanage, where he probably didn't last long, either.

So off went Anne and Mary, back to prison, where Mary died of a fever before giving birth. As for Anne, although it's known that she was never hanged, her ending is a mystery. The most likely theory is that her long-suffering father used his influence to spring her. What happened after that is anybody's guess. Theories that she returned to her father or her husband, or even that she became a nun, are unlikely. I like to imagine that she opened a little tavern

in the Bahamas, frequented by rough men who sported bandan-
nas, wooden legs, and eye patches, and maybe there she met a man
called Long John Silver. . . .

PIRATE QUEEN POP CULTURE

You'd think there would be tons of movies about someone as
famous as Anne Bonny, but my research has turned up pretty
poor pickings. The most likely flick is a little pearl from 1951 called
Anne of the Indies, directed by the great Jacques Tourneur, who
also gave us classic horror movies and noir thrillers like *I Walked
with a Zombie, Cat People,* and *Out of the Past.*

Anne of the Indies stars Jean Peters as pirate Anne, a thinly
disguised Anne Bonny character, who, like the real Anne, dresses
herself up as a man. This film sometimes plays on late night—
or very early morning—TV. Look for it!

Grania O'Malley had even less luck. The one movie I found
that might have been inspired by her is the dismal 1961 Italian
Queen of the Pirates. The only real similarities between *Queen of
the Pirates* and Grania herself are that the movie takes place in the
same century that Grania lived, and both the heroine and her
father are pirates. Except everybody in the film is Italian! Don't
even bother looking for *Queen of the Pirates;* it can't be found

in even the most esoteric of video stores and is never on television.

On the other hand, Anne Bonny was the sweetheart of comic books. A 1947 comic called *It Really Happened* tells Anne's story nicely in "Lady of the Black Flag." A 1949 comic book is called *Captain Kidd,* but despite the name it relates Anne's adventures

Anne Bonny and Mary Read defend their ship. A little bit of historic accuracy from the 1940s comic, "The Sorceress of the Briny Deep."

in a story called "The Sorceress of the Briny Deep." No detail of Anne's life is left out of the story, even to young Anne stabbing her maid, but the unknown writer, obviously unsatisfied with Anne's disappearance from history, decided to write his own ending. On the comic's last page Anne, out of jail, goes back to piracy, trips over a loose rope on deck, falls overboard—and drowns!

Lola Montez

It was the evening of June 3, 1843, and an A-list of aristocrats, dandies, and swells jammed into Her Majesty's Theater in London, to witness the debut of *Doña Lola Montez of the Teatro Real, Seville, For the First Time on Any English Stage.*

The curtain rose on a Moorish backdrop. On center stage stood an incredibly lovely young woman, jet black curls cascading to her white shoulders, dark eyes glowing. Women in the audience, fanning themselves in the crowded theater, murmured, "She's so—so *Spanish!*" As the orchestra struck up a bolero, "El Olaño," she began to dance, hips swaying, castanets clicking. According to one poetic journalist, "Lithe and graceful as a young fawn, every movement that she made seemed instinct with melody ... as she swept around the stage, her slender waist swayed to the music and her graceful neck and head bent with it, like a flower that bends with the impulse given to its stem by the wind."

The dance ended, La Montez curtsied low, and there was a silence from the audience—the kind of silence that is usually followed by tumultuous applause—when from out of the hush rose the voice of one Lord Ravetagh, exclaiming, "Good grief, it's Betty James!"

Eliza Roseanna Gilbert was born in Limerick, Ireland, in 1821. Her twenty-year-old father was a captain in the King's Own Scottish Borders, and her beautiful fifteen-year-old mother, also named Eliza, was an illegitimate daughter of Charles Oliver, from a wealthy Irish family. When little Eliza was four years old, her father was sent to India, taking his family with him. When he died from cholera three years later, the elder Eliza Gilbert married her late husband's best friend, sent her daughter off to London to live with relatives, and didn't return to claim her until 1837.

At this point, fifteen-year-old Eliza the younger was creating a sensation in Bath with her fresh, dark-eyed beauty. Mama promptly engaged her daughter to a very rich seventy-year-old man named Sir Abraham Lumley. When she told Eliza that Sir Abraham had given his promise, the girl replied, "At seventy, what can a man promise?" and eloped with the nearest handy young man, Thomas James (hence the name "Betty James"), who also happened to be one of her mother's many admirers.

The couple moved to Calcutta, where Eliza's looks created the same sensation among the British community there as they had caused in Bath. Emily Eden, sister of the British viceroy, wrote in her journal, "Simla is much moved just now by the arrival of a Mrs. James who has been talked of as the great beauty of the year. . . . At present the husband and wife appear very fond of each other, but a girl who marries at fifteen hardly knows what she likes."

Emily Eden was right. Eliza soon grew bored with her husband and tried returning home to Ireland and Mama. When that didn't work out—thirty years old and still lovely, Eliza the elder resented the competition from Eliza the younger—she headed back to England. A shipboard affair with one Mr. Lennox, which Thomas James got wind of, resulted in Eliza being faced with divorce proceedings upon her arrival.

Finding herself alone and friendless in England, there was only one thing to do. Eliza traveled to Madrid, studied for four months under a Spanish teacher, and returned to England as Lola Montez, renowned Spanish dancer, born in Seville.

From London, Lola, as we shall now call her, went to Brussels, Poland, Russia, and France. Her early successes were uneven, and she played sometimes to sold-out crowds, sometimes to empty theaters. At one point she ran out of money and was reduced to singing in the streets for coins. She always bounced back, and there was always some handsome, kindly, rich gentleman to give her a hand when she needed it. In Russia, she had a brief affair with Tsar Nicholas IV, and in Dresden, she had an affair with the famous composer Franz Liszt. But Lola wanted security. She told a friend, "The moment I get a nice sum of money, I am going to try to hook a prince."

And that's what she did. She headed for Germany, where thirty-six tiny kingdoms boasted thirty-six different kings. You couldn't swing a cat without hitting a prince. She met Prince Henry of Reuss (I never heard of Reuss either), and became his mistress. That didn't last long. Lola had a hard time obeying court etiquette, and finally tried the prince's patience by treading all over his prized pansies. And so it was, so long, Reuss, hello Bavaria—and hello, King Ludwig of Bavaria.

The king was sixty-one years old, Lola was a luscious twenty-five. He hired her to "teach him Spanish," and she taught him a lot more than that. The grateful king paid her 20,000 florins a year, made her the Countess of Landesfeld, and built a magnificent palace for her. She was even made a Cannoness of the Order of Saint Theresa!

But the peasants were revolting, and they weren't too crazy about their king's mistress, either. In 1848, Ludwig was forced to abdicate the throne, and Lola was banished. She picked herself up, dusted herself off, and started all over again. Europe was so *over!* She sailed for America and Gold Rush country, taking with her Ludwig's jewels, her Louis XVI cabinets, her swan bed, her billiard table, and her pet bear. In San Francisco and the rough'n'-tumble mining towns, she presented her latest entertainment, the Spider Dance. This was a kind of tarantula tarantella, and it consisted of Lola gyrating around the stage while shaking rubber spiders out of her costume (I am not making this up). They loved her! When Lola inched her skirt up on her shapely legs, looking

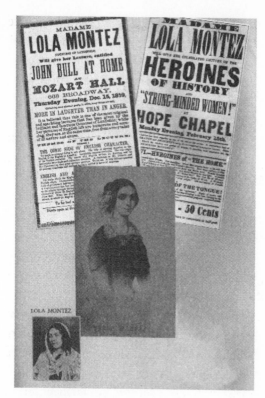

for spiders that had strayed further than the bounds of propriety, the boys in the back row would shout, "Higher! Higher!"

The truth is that Lola was not really much of a dancer, but she *was* a first-rate babe, which was enough for all those woman-starved miners. Anyway, you had to be careful about criticizing Lola. She horsewhipped at least one reporter who had given her a bad review, and she challenged another to a duel.

If she didn't always have the greatest relationship with the press, there were exceptions. In 1853, Lola and Patrick Purdy Hall, owner and editor of the San Francisco *Whig*, were married at San Francisco's Mission Dolores. Like all her other relationships, this one didn't last.

But Lola was ready for a lasting relationship with California. She moved to a cottage in Grass Valley, a small town nestled in the California Sierras, planning to retire and live the simple life, surrounded by, as a reporter from the San Francisco *Herald* wrote, "her pet birds, dogs, goats, sheep, hens, and turkeys; and her pony, a favorite and constant companion in all her mountain rambles." One wonders what happened to the bear.

There Lola might have happily stayed, except that a forest fire burned down her house, destroying everything, including Ludwig's jewels, the Louis XVI cabinets, the swan bed, and the billiard table. The irrepressible Lola bounced back once again, sailing to Australia to star in her own play, *Lola Montez in Bavaria*. Then it was back to Europe, finally even touring her home country, Ireland.

By this time, the first flush of youth was long gone, along with her incredible beauty. As befitted a mature woman, Lola had said good-bye to dancing, and instead went on lecture tours, often under her more aristocratic title, the Countess of Landesfeld. Her subjects varied from the differences between Brits and Yanks, to "Heroines of History and Strong-Minded Women!" She had gotten serious. In 1858 she wrote and published three (!) books: *The Arts of Beauty, or Secrets of a Lady's Toilette With Hints to Gentlemen on the Art of Fascination, Anecdotes of Love; Being True Accounts of the Most Remarkable Events Connected With the History of Love; in All Ages and Among All Nations*, and *Lectures of Lola Montez, Including Her Autobiography.*

As Lola's looks left her, she became more and more interested in spiritualism, finally returning to America to lecture on the subject at "Hope Chapel," in New York. Unfortunately, the lectures were failures; both the press and the public took the notorious La Montez with a great deal of salt. Seriously broke, her luck held one more time, when she met an old girlfriend who was now married to a New York florist. The couple took care of Lola, who by now had become deeply religious. With no financial worries, Lola spent her time reading the Bible and pursuing spiritualism.

She died of tuberculosis in 1861, at the young age of forty-three. Over a period of forty years, she had survived by continually reinventing herself, and had been the most outrageous, if not the most approved of, woman of her time.

THEY DIDN'T ALL STAY IN IRELAND

Lola Montez was hardly the first Irish rose to transplant herself in the New World. Between 1847 and 1854, more than one and a quarter million Irish emigrated to America. Between 1851 and 1901, another three million crossed the Atlantic to the land of opportunity. It's a wonder there were any Irish left in Ireland.

Of those millions of Irish, more than half were women. The majority came over during and after the Great Potato Famine in mid-century, choosing emigration over starvation. And most of them were single women, traveling alone. They found work in the factories, as seamstresses and as teachers, but mostly they wound up as housemaids, working for room and board, and $1.50 per week. It was better than starving in Ireland.

Most of them were "nice girls"—the virtue of Irish women was almost legendary—but there was the occasional infamous immigrant like Maria Sullivan, who ran a brothel in Massachusetts, or Bridget Fury and Irish Mary, madames who dabbled in robbery on the side.

None of them ever became a superstar like Lola Montez.

Irish immigrant women in New York, late nineteenth century.

PART THREE

KATHLEEN NI HOULIHAN

After Dervorgilla's lover invited the British into Ireland, the Irish spent the next seven hundred years trying to get them out again. Queen Elizabeth tightened England's hold on Ireland by evicting Irish landowners and moving in British subjects. Nonetheless, just as she had pardoned Grania O'Malley, she was smart enough to pardon her adversary, Hugh O'Neill, who had fought for Ireland's independence and lost. When "the O'Neill," as he was called, learned of Elizabeth's death, he wept aloud.

Liz knew how to turn her enemies into friends. The same cannot be said of the Puritan dictator Oliver Cromwell. Like all fanatics, he believed God was on his side, and he invented ethnic cleansing in his attempt to destroy as many Irish

Catholics as possible. It almost worked. Thousands of men, women, and children were slaughtered by his armies. He burned Catholic churches, forbade the celebration of mass, and put a price of £5 each on the heads of Catholic priests.

Cromwell was finally beheaded, but that didn't stop things from going from bad to worse in Ireland. Irish Catholics no longer owned their own land; they had to pay rent to their Anglo landlords. Any attempt to improve their land led to an increase in rent. Catholics weren't allowed to vote, or even to own a horse that was worth more than £5. The Catholic Church was simply not recognized. Catholic priests were outlawed, and the bounty on their heads was raised to £20. The Irish language was suppressed, and the only education that most Irish children got came from itinerant teachers who wandered from village to village, setting up classes in hedges and fields, often in exchange for meals.

Because poor farmers usually had to sell all their crops to pay their rents, they wound up living on potatoes, which were easy to grow and could feed their families. In 1845, a blight destroyed the nation's potato crops. This was the beginning of the Great Potato Famine, and before it ended in 1851, millions of people had died of starvation, and millions more had fled to America.

England did nothing to help. In fact, the British government was delighted. The London *Times* reported that "an Irishman will soon be as rare a sight in Connemara as a Red Indian on the shores of Manhattan."

Revolutions start when things have gotten so bad that there's nothing left to lose, and this is what happened in Ireland. The Irish had been fighting for their freedom for centuries, but this time the physical revolution was combined with a cultural revolution: a revival of Irish folklore, myths, poetry, and language. It was this Irish renaissance that produced a new breed of woman warrior, beautiful and strong as her mythic counterpart, who fought for Ireland's freedom—sometimes on the cultural front, like Lady Gregory, Maud Gonne, and Hazel Lavery, or armed with a real working gun and wearing a uniform, like Countess Markievicz. These women were born Protestant and rich, and they could have chosen parties and ballgowns over revolution, but Ireland was in their hearts. Chronicling them in his poetry, like a turn-of-the-century bard, was the poet William Butler Yeats, friend and collaborator with all and in love with at least one.

Important note: In the following section of the book, when I use the word Republican, I am not referring to the party of Richard Nixon, Ronald Reagan, and George Bush. "Republicans" were those Irish nationalists who wanted their country to be a republic, free of England.

LITERARY ROSES

Lady Wilde, "Speranza"

In September 1845, the first year of the Great Potato Famine, a beautiful teenaged girl named Jane Francesca Elgee watched through her window as a long, imposing funeral cortege passed her house in Dublin. What important person was being buried? she wished to know. It was the funeral of Thomas Davis, dead at the age of thirty-one: poet, political writer, and cofounder of *The Nation*, an ardently pro-Irish weekly newspaper.

Jane came from a respectable Protestant family. Her father was a successful lawyer; her grandfather had been the archdeacon of Wexford. She was well-educated, and in fact had insisted on an education, telling her governess, "If you won't educate me, I'll educate myself."

Jane could have lived the carefree life of any other rich Protestant girl in Dublin—riding, hunting, and going to parties—but she was a regular reader of *The Nation*, and had read Davis's passionate arguments for a return to the Irish language, history, and literature, which he had published under the pseudonym, "The Celt."

Inspired by Davis, Jane began contributing her own fiercely nationalistic poetry and prose to *The Nation*, under the pen name

Speranza, Italian for "hope." Yet her angry poem, "The Famine Year," about starving Irish peasants evicted from their homes to die on the road, is hardly full of hope:

> *Oh! We know not what is smiling,*
> *and we know not what is dying;*
> *But we're hungry, very hungry, and*
> *we cannot stop our crying.*

The poem ends with her desire for a divine punishment:

Speranza.

> *But God will yet take vengeance for*
> *the souls for whom Christ died . . .*
> *A ghastly spectral army, before great God we'll stand,*
> *And arraign ye as our murderers, O spoilers of our land!*

Speranza's writing grew more militant, and soon, instead of calling upon God for vengeance, she called to the people of Ireland for action:

> Ireland! Ireland! It is no petty insurrection . . . that summons you to the field. . . . It is a death struggle between the oppressor and the slave. . . . Strike! Strike!

A week later, she wrote:

> Oh! For a hundred thousand muskets glittering brightly
> in the light of heaven . . . in the name then of your trampled,
> degraded country . . . I call on you to make this aspiration
> of your souls a deed.

This time she went too far. She was calling for armed rebellion. The government destroyed all issues of *The Nation* they could get their hands on, and arrested editor Gavan Duffy. Jane stood up and proudly proclaimed that she was Speranza.

Speranza was a woman! Thrilled, the educated, well-off people of Ireland loved her, and the tall, dark-haired beauty made converts to her cause. As for Duffy, the British government tried him for treason nine times, and each time he was acquitted. He wound up elected to British Parliament and organized a tenant's union to help evicted Irish farmers.

In 1851, Jane married eye surgeon and folklorist Sir William Wilde, and became Lady Wilde. Four years later, she gave birth to Oscar Fingal O'Flahertie Wilde. She had named little Oscar after one of the heroes in Irish mythology: Oscar, of Finn MacCool's Fennians.

Sir William died in 1876, and Jane took Oscar and his brother William to London, and started writing about folklore. Finally answering Thomas Davis's call for a return to Irish history and legend, she published *Ancient Legends of Ireland* in 1887. Her home became a salon for such literary figures as George Bernard Shaw and William Butler Yeats, and she herself was an inspiration for these young writers. All told, Lady Wilde wrote six books during her lifetime, and translated many others.

The beautiful young Speranza who had so inflamed Ireland was by now a corpulent fiftysomething who bore an uncanny resemblance to son Oscar in drag. A woman who visited Lady Wilde while she still lived in Dublin described her bohemian way of dressing: "The old-fashioned purple brocade gown, the towering head-dress of velvet . . . innumerable and enormous brooches . . . huge bracelets of turquoise and gold . . . rings on every finger."

Oscar Wilde, all grown up now, was at that time editing a magazine called *The Woman's World*. Originally called *The Lady's World*, it had been a fashion magazine that featured articles about nothing more important than the season's hats. Under Oscar's editorship, it became a feminist magazine for educated women, and Mom was one of the chief contributors. In a nod to the magazine's earlier incarnation as a fashion magazine, Lady Wilde, the eccentric dresser, wrote about clothing reform:

> The literary dress should be free, untrammeled and unswathed, as simple and as easily adjusted as Greek drapery . . . and the fewer frills, cuffs, cascades of lace, the better,

for in moments of divine frenzy or feverish excitement the authoress is prone to overturn her ink-bottle.

In 1895, Oscar was put on trial for what he called "the love that dare not speak its name." Friends advised him to get out of England while the getting was good, but Lady Wilde, ever the believer in fighting for justice, and amazingly liberal for those days, wanted him to stay and fight. She told him, "If you stay, even if you go to prison, you will always be my son. It will make no difference to my affection."

Oscar stayed, was found guilty of homosexuality, and was sent to prison. Her heart broken, Lady Wilde died in 1896. Had she hung on for a few years longer, she would have seen the full flowering of the Irish literary renaissance, sprung from seeds she planted.

Lady Wilde in her later years.

LIKE MOTHER, LIKE SON

Oscar Wilde had a trial that shocked British society; his mother had a trial that shocked Dublin society.

Sir William Wilde was, plain and simply, a bounder, who reportedly populated half of Ireland with his illegitimate children. George Bernard Shaw wrote about him: "He was currently reported to have a family in every farmhouse; and the wonder was that Lady Wilde didn't mind...."

Sir William met his match in the person of one Mary Josephine Travers, the thirtysomething daughter of another prominent physician. In 1862, she'd been cured by Sir William of deafness, and the two became close friends. How close? Well, he lent her books—and money—and escorted her to such rousing affairs as the meeting of the British Association, the Dublin Exhibition, and lectures at Trinity College. Too close, thought Lady Wilde, who expressed her disapproval—tongues were wagging, she said—but the relationship continued.

Then one day Sir William made a pass at Mary. According to Mary's later testimony, she called him "a spiteful old lunatic," and stormed out. Sir William bombarded her with letters of apology, and sent her "pretty bonnets and warm underclothing," all of which she returned. He wrote, "Are we to meet no more? I have bought you a dark gray dress with brown velvet trimmings."

Eventually, Mary forgave Sir William long enough to ask for, and get, money to pay her fare to Australia. She got as far as Liverpool, changed her mind, returned to Dublin, and resumed their friendship, despite the fact that he "attempted the most unbecoming liberties, and even found fault with her bonnet."

Somewhere along the way, according to Mary, Sir William doped her and had his way with her. The relationship continued, as did Sir William's loans of money. According to Mary, he simply *insisted* that she accept the money.

God only knows why, but Mary decided to visit Lady Wilde, who of course refused to see her. Could she have hoped the lady would divorce her husband, so that she, Mary, could become the next Lady Wilde? She wrote letters to Lady Wilde, all about her affair with Sir William. They were returned with a note: "The enclosed is returned, as Lady Wilde does not take the least interest in the subject." She sent a photo of herself to Sir William, which Lady Wilde mailed back to her with another note: "Dear Miss Travers, Dr. Wilde returns your photograph. Yours very truly, Jane Wilde."

At this point Mary started obsessing on Lady Wilde. She began by giving her books bad reviews, describing her newest book, *The First Temptation,* as "blasphemous work, treating religious matters with abominable frivolity."

Bad reviews were not enough: Mary's next step was to pub-lish a booklet called *Florence Boyle Price: or A Warning,* which she signed with Lady Wilde's pseudonym, Speranza. In the book, a thinly disguised Mary, "lonely and unsophisticated," is drugged and raped by the family doctor. She stalked Sir William, selling her book at his various lectures.

Finally Lady Wilde had enough. She sent a letter to Mary's father:

> *Sir,*
>
> *You may not be aware of the disreputable conduct of your daughter at Bray, where she consorts with all the low newspaper boys in the place, employing them to disseminate offensive placards in which my name is given, and also tracts in which she makes it appear that she has an intrigue with Sir William Wilde.*

The letter went on to accuse Mary of trying to get money from Sir William and Lady Wilde. Dr. Travers couldn't have been too concerned; maybe he was used to his daughter's behavior. He read the letter and filed it away in his desk. Mary took it out, read it, and sued Lady Wilde for libel. She wanted £2,000.

The trial was gleefully covered by the British press, which annoyed the Irish press no end. An Irish newspaper, the *Freeman's*

Journal, wrote, "All we ask is that our English critics will allow us to settle our own affairs."

At one point, the defending lawyer asked Mary, "You adopted Lady Wilde's pen-name of 'Speranza.' Was that to annoy her?"

"Well," answered Mary, "she had no right to the name."

Finally the jury turned in their verdict: Well, okay, maybe Lady Wilde's letter was a teensy bit libelous. And they awarded Mary one farthing, which was what she was worth.

Lady Wilde and Sir William.

Lady Gregory

In 1896, the same year that Lady Wilde died, a young poet met a forty-four-year-old widow at her mansion in Coole Park, near Galway, and Ireland changed forever.

Isabella Augusta Persse became Lady Gregory at the age of twenty-seven, when she married Sir William Gregory, former governor of Ceylon, former privy councilor, and thirty-five years her senior. Some histories of the couple depict their marriage as happy; I don't think so. Young Augusta, largely ignored by her Protestant mother—who did have, after all, fifteen *other* children to deal with, and anyway, was disappointed that Augusta was not a boy—spent most of her childhood years with her Irish Catholic nurse, who reared her on stories of old Ireland and the ancient heroes and rebellions. As Lady Gregory, she even asked one of her husband's gardeners to teach her Irish, but he thought she was making fun of him. What educated Anglo-Protestant of the day would want to learn the despised language of the lower classes?

Sir William, on the other hand, was all Anglo stuff and snobbery. After the Great Famine, he had proposed the "congested districts" scheme, the gist of which was that any farm smaller than a quarter-acre couldn't pay for itself, so the smallest, and therefore poorest, farmers were evicted. He dragged his new wife along to tour the museums of Europe, making her leave her dearly beloved two-month-old son behind with a nanny. Their friends were her husband's friends, elderly and conservative.

Lady Gregory fulfilled the role of dutiful Victorian wife up to a point. She wrote and published some poetry, although not anywhere near the tremendous outpouring she would produce after her husband's death, and she had affairs. One affair, which lasted at least a year, was with poet and Irish nationalist Wilfrid Blunt, who had gone to prison for his beliefs. She proofread his poems, and he published her book of poetry in 1891, modestly titled *Sonnets by a Woman.* In memory of their romance, she pasted his photograph into the book of his poetry that he'd given her.

Wilfrid Blunt was also married at the time, and he had already had an affair with Jane Morris, who was married to the Pre-Raphaelite poet and artist William Morris. These Victorians were not as stuffy as we've been led to believe.

Sir William died in 1892, and Lady Gregory, aged forty, wore black for the rest of her life. She also finally came alive. Visiting the cottages of Galway, she started collecting Irish folklore, histories, and legends. Then, that summer of 1896, Lady Gregory's neighbor, playwright Edward Martyn, brought William Butler Yeats over for lunch. Yeats was already a superstar poet who wrote yearning, Pre-Raphaelite-style poems about the misty magic of ancient Ireland. Four years earlier, he had cofounded, with the beautiful activist Maud Gonne, the Irish Literary Society, which brought libraries and Irish culture to the villages and towns of the countryside.

Over lunch, Martyn complained about the difficulty he was having getting his plays produced. There was no Irish theater, and London could care less about the work of this Catholic writer who stressed Irish tradition and culture in his writings. Like *fin de siècle* Mickey Rooneys and Judy Garlands, Lady Gregory and Yeats got an idea: Let's start a theater and put on our own plays!

And they did. The Irish Literary Theater, which eventually moved into the old Mechanics Institute building on Abbey Street, became the Abbey Theater. Their first produced play, on May 8, 1899, was Yeats's *The Countess Kathleen,* about the legendary countess who sold her soul to the devil to win back the souls of her people. Martyn, not as famous, had to wait for the next day to see his play, *The Heather Field,* staged.

Lady Gregory became director of the theater and friend, collaborator, and patroness not only to Yeats, but to writers like J. M. Synge, Sean O'Casey, and George Bernard Shaw. In the tradition of Lady Wilde, her home at Coole Park was open to all the writers of the Irish renaissance, as were her purse strings—none of her guests was rich, and she didn't mind sharing Sir William's bounty. She would have liked to have been more than friends with

Yeats, but he'd given his heart to Maud Gonne, his muse for life. The dowdy Augusta, twenty years older than Yeats, knew she didn't have a chance, and she got pretty catty about the situation. After meeting the famous beauty in 1898, Augusta wrote about Maud: "Instead of beauty I saw a death's head."

Lady Gregory and Yeats inspired each other, and she set to work in earnest. By the age of fifty, she had mastered the Irish language. From 1900 to 1903, she recorded ancient Irish sagas. Her three years of labor resulted in *Cuchulainn of Muirthemne*, her retelling of the Cuchulain myth, published in 1902. From 1903 on, she published a collection of Irish folklore every few years for the rest of her life. She made what was for a proper Protestant an amazing discovery: in her memoirs, she writes, "We found startling beliefs and came to the conclusion that Ireland is Pagan, not Xtian (Christian)."

And she discovered drama, eventually becoming the most popular Irish playwright of her time. All told, Lady Gregory wrote forty plays in her lifetime, but was never officially credited with the most important of them all, *Kathleen Ni Houlihan*, her collaboration with Yeats.

Kathleen Ni Houlihan, which was inspired by one of Yeats's dreams, combines two traditional female personifications of Ireland: the Shan Van Vocht, the poor old woman, and Kathleen Ni Houlihan, the beautiful girl. A poor old woman, roaming the

Lady Gregory.

countryside, stops at a house where a wedding is taking place, and bewitches the groom so that he leaves his bride and goes off to fight for Ireland. By the end of the play—just like the ancient war goddess, the Morrigan, who could change from hag to lovely maiden—the Shan Van Vocht turns into beautiful Kathleen Ni Houlihan, Ireland personified as a queen. After thousands of years, Ireland and the Morrigan had become one again.

Although she never said anything publicly about it, Augusta was bitter that Yeats never gave her credit for the play. Years later, she wrote in her diary, "Rather hard on me not giving my name with *Kathleen Ni Houlihan* that I wrote all but all of."

Neither Augusta nor Yeats was prepared for the political fervor their play inspired. When the curtain fell, the audience spontaneously burst into song, singing nationalist Ireland's unofficial anthem, "A Nation Once Again." Stunned, Yeats wondered "if such plays should be produced unless one was prepared for people to go out to shoot or be shot. . . ."

Lady Gregory, who at first had simply cared about restoring Ireland's culture, became a revolutionary. In the late 'teens, with Ireland suffering under a repressive British occupation, she and a group of actresses leaving the Abbey Theater were confronted by the Black and Tans, the British military police named for their dark green, almost black, tunics and tan trousers. Leveling guns on the women, the cops demanded they put their hands in the air.

The frightened actresses threw themselves on the ground, but Augusta, in her mid-sixties now, stood tall, shouting, "Up the rebels!"

In 1922, Ireland and England signed a treaty, making Ireland the equivalent of Canada, a self-governing nation, but still under British rule. The signing of the treaty started a yearlong civil war between the pro-treaty factions and the anti-treaty factions, who refused to compromise, wanting a completely independent Ireland. Augusta lined herself up with the anti-treaty group, stating, "I wish to put myself on the side of the people, I wish to go to prison, I think even to execution. . . ."

But of course nobody was about to execute Lady Augusta Gregory, Ireland's greatest treasure. She died of breast cancer at the age of eighty.

SHE WAS STILL A VICTORIAN

Despite her numerous love affairs, Lady Gregory was a woman of her time, and in her retelling of the Cuchulain myth, she left out parts that she, or possibly her publisher, deemed unsuitable for proper Victorian eyes. Thus, many of the earthier stories, such as Dervorgilla's pissing contest, can't be found in *Cuchulainn of Muirthemne.* Also missing from Lady Gregory's book is the information that when the warrior queen Maeve peed, the force of her urine was such that it washed three deep trenches, each big enough to hold a house, into the soil. That sexually insatiable queen had the biggest bladder of all. Her bodily fluids could either be life giving, as when she peed the three lakes full of water, or destructive. Another time that she peed, the force of her urine washed away everything—grass, bushes, even trees—leaving nothing but bare earth and great boulders. And forever after, that place was called *Mun Medhbi,* "Maeve's Urine."

Muses of the Irish Renaissance

Maud Gonne

If Maud Gonne had not existed, William Butler Yeats would have had to invent her. She was his muse, the inspiration for much of his poetry and plays, his lifelong—and unconsummated—love. For him, and for the people of Ireland, she was Kathleen Ni Houlihan, a personification of their country, and the Irish Joan of Arc.

Maud Gonne could have had anything she wanted. She was rich, born to an Irish father who was a colonel in the British Army, tall—at the age of sixteen, she was already 5'10"—and beautiful, with golden hair and golden eyes. She was the belle of Dublin society.

But what she wanted was to be a rebel, socially as well as politically. At the age of twenty, so she later told Yeats, she made a bargain with the devil for control over her own life. The next year, in Paris, she started an affair with the married French writer, Lucien Milevoye. You can imagine the scandal, but Maud couldn't care less. Her father had died and left her £20,000. She could afford to flout convention.

In 1889, she met Yeats. She was twenty-two, he was twenty-three, and it was love at first sight—for him, but not for Maud, who still had her French lover. In 1891, their one-year-old son,

Georges, died of meningitis, and an inconsolable Maud, unable to sleep without using chloroform, swathed herself in black and sailed back to Ireland. Yeats was there to meet her ship and to make an attempt at consoling her. They smoked hashish together, and he got her interested in mysticism. In 1890, he had joined the mystic Rosicrucian Order of the Golden Dawn. Now Maud joined it, too. Yeats also proposed to her, for the first of three times. She turned him down. She even conceded that she and "Willie" were spiritually married, but that was as far as she would go.

The Order of the Golden Dawn was unusual, even for occult organizations, in that the women who belonged to it were considered the equal of the men. Feminist Maud loved it, but her leanings were toward action, revolution, and the future of Ireland, while mystic Yeats was rooted in the romantic, Pre-Raphaelite past, what he dubbed his "Celtic Twilight."

For Maud, Yeats became an activist. He marched in demonstrations led by her and called her "the New Speranza." Together they formed the Irish Literary Society. Together they organized an anti-English protest on Queen Victoria's sixtieth birthday. Together they joined the Irish Republican Brotherhood, which years later would become the Irish Republican Army.

Yeats wrote poetry about Maud, and plays for her to act in. In 1892, she played the title role in *The Countess Kathleen*, the first play produced by the Abbey Theater. Ten years later, she played another Kathleen, the personification of Ireland, *Kathleen Ni Houlihan*. With that role, Maud became identified forever as the living representation of Ireland, a flesh-and-blood goddess.

The two were a famous couple. Ella Young, Irish writer and folklorist (whom Yeats had *also* once proposed to) described people's reactions when Maud and Willie walked down the streets of Dublin together: "It is Maud Gonne and the Poet. She has a radiance as of sunlight. Yeats, that leopard of the moon, holds back in a leash a huge lion-colored Great Dane—Maud Gonne's dog, Dagda."

In 1910, Yeats wrote the poem, "Another Troy," describing his unhappiness at Maud's rejection of his love, and his disapproval of her political activism, which he felt was wasted on common-ers. Mistakenly, I think, he compares her to Helen of Troy (the newspapers, more aptly called her the Irish Joan of Arc), asking "Was there another Troy for her to burn?" Although her name is never mentioned in the poem, all of Ireland knew that "her" referred to Maud Gonne.

Meanwhile, in 1894, Maud had borne another child to Lucien—a girl, this time. Some whispered that little Iseult had been con-ceived in the catacombs beneath Georges's burial vault. In 1896, Yeats had tried to console himself by having an affair with the writer Olivia Shakespear. That lasted about a year, but Maud's phantom kept getting in the way. Finally, as he wrote in "The

Lover Mourns for the Loss of Love," Olivia looked into his heart, saw Maud's image there, and went "weeping away."

Yeats proposed to Maud again, and was rejected again, in 1899. He busied himself with his poetry, and she with her activism. She cofounded a suffragist women's society, the Daughters of Erin, and wrote feminist articles for the organization's magazine. In 1903, she married Major John MacBride, another Irish national-ist. They had a son, Sean, but their marriage was a disaster, ending in divorce. John MacBride turned out to be an alcoholic and a vio-lent man who molested Maud's daughter. MacBride was one of the leaders of the ill-fated 1916 Easter Rising, when a small band of revolutionaries managed to occupy Dublin for a week. He was executed by the British for his part in the rebellion, and Yeats, in his poem, "Easter, 1916," writes that even though MacBride was a "drunken, vainglorious lout," his death made him a martyr, and that he, like the other martyrs of the rebellion, was "transformed utterly."

Then Yeats proposed to the newly widowed Maud for a third time.

And was rejected.

In desperation, the next year he proposed to Maud's now twenty-three-year-old daughter, Iseult, who also rejected him. Finally, in 1918, he gave up the Gonnes and married Georgie Hyde-Lees.

Maud Gonne, Ireland's lovely Joan of Arc.

Maud, Ireland's living goddess, continued to follow the path of the warrior queen. A year after John McBride was executed, she was arrested by the British for her activism and spent six months in prison. In 1922, when Ireland signed a compromise treaty with Britain, Maud, like Lady Gregory, was on the anti-treaty side. Yeats, always more conservative than the women, sided with the new pro-treaty Irish Free State and was elected to the Senate.

Maud, the firebrand, was imprisoned by the Irish Free State, Yeats' government, in 1923. She and ninety-one other activist women promptly went on a hunger strike, and were released after twenty days.

Yeats never got over Maud. At the age of sixty, he wrote "Among School Children," a poem about his visit to an Irish school. He has become, he writes, "A sixty year old smiling public man." But in the poem, he suddenly remembers Maud telling him a story about her childhood, and in his mind's eye, sees her standing there before him "as a living child."

Willie died in 1939; Maud hung on till 1953. Some good came of her short marriage to the boorish martyr John MacBride: their son, Sean, won the Nobel Peace Prize and founded Amnesty International.

A 1910 caricature of Yeats, by American woman cartoonist Kate Carew.

EASTER REBELLION 101

It was a beautiful gesture, and it was doomed, but on Easter Monday 1916, a small group of about a thousand volunteers invaded Dublin, took over key buildings, and held the city for nearly a week.

The rebellion's leaders were schoolmasters and poets. With the exception of Commandant-General James Connolly, none of them had military experience. Due to really lousy communication, the original plan—for uprisings all over Ireland—fell through. Due to even worse communication, nobody was there to meet the German ship that was loaded with guns for the revolution, so the ship sat in the waters off Kerry for three days before the ship's captain, threatened by British soldiers, scuttled it.

The next day, England sent in 6,500 soldiers. The civilian army didn't have a chance in a million, but they held out for six days before Connolly, his ankle shattered by a bullet and in great pain, decided to surrender and save the lives of what was left of the rebels.

You can't have a revolution without the support of the people you're fighting for, and the rebels had no support. When Commander-in-Chief Padraic Pearse, standing on the front steps of the post office building, read the Proclamation of the Republic to a crowd of citizens, the people were hopelessly confused. What rebellion? They knew nothing about it. After the surrender, jeering crowds threw rotten vegetables at the tattered, exhausted prisoners.

Alone in their prison cells, waiting for the firing squad, the prisoners wrote poetry. Public opinion turned around 180 degrees after sixteen of the rebellion's leaders were executed. Too late, the people of Ireland realized what the rebels had tried to do for them.

Yeats described the rebellion as "a terrible beauty" and wrote that Ireland was "changed, changed utterly." He was right. The Easter Rebellion, doomed from the start, was the first battle in a war that would finally end with Ireland's independence.

Lady Hazel Lavery

If you've ever looked at an Irish pound note printed between 1927 and 1976, you've seen Hazel Lavery, though you may not have known it. She is the beautiful woman in the oval, representing the spirit of Erin, Kathleen Ni Houlihan. A shawl covering her hair, her body faces the future, but she gazes symbolically back at the past.

Born in Chicago, on March 14, 1880, debutante Hazel Martyn had been named "the most beautiful girl in the Midwest" before

Hazel Lavery as Kathleen Ni Houlihan, on the old Irish pound note.

she turned sixteen. Hazel's Irish American father, Edward Martyn, a typical American self-made man, had earned his fortune at the Armour meat company in the city known as "hog butcher of the world." Edward died when Hazel was seventeen, but she had grown up on tales of his Irish ancestry, which went way back to thirteenth-century Galway.

Hazel had a talent for art, which Mama Alice didn't mind encouraging. Of course she expected that her daughter, like any proper society girl, would eventually find a suitable husband, and art would become a hobby. In this case, the "suitable husband" was tall, dark, and handsome Dr. Ned Trudeau, whom Hazel had met while attending finishing school. The courtship was one-sided. Although Mama approved, Hazel wasn't interested.

Alice took her daughter on painting and sketching trips to France, where Hazel got a taste of the bohemian life. When Hazel met, and seemed attracted to, famous Belfast-born society painter John Lavery at a Brittany artists' colony in 1903, Alice grew alarmed. For all his success and fame, John was a widower with a grown daughter, and he was twice Hazel's age. She sent a telegram to Ned: "Come quick or you'll lose Hazel."

Ned caught the next liner to France. In light of all those past Irish roses who waded through hell to get the men they loved, Hazel seems a bit of a wimp, because despite evidence that she really loved John Lavery—she sent him tearstained letters bemoaning the fact that they had to part—she let Alice convince her to marry Ned.

It was a huge, expensive, New York society wedding, covered by the press. The bride was lovely in white satin and orange blossoms, and had a broken heart. But within four months, Ned was dead of pneumonia, contracted during an epidemic. Pregnant Hazel returned to Chicago, took back her maiden name, and gave birth to a daughter, whom she named Alice, after Mama. And she resumed writing to John Lavery.

Mama Alice and Hazel bounced back and forth between Chicago and Europe during the next few years. Hazel met with John secretly, because Alice still disapproved. Finally, in 1909, Mama Alice died, and Hazel was free to marry John. She was twenty-six, he was fifty-three. Daughter Alice was bridesmaid.

The new family moved into John's Regency house in London's fashionable South Kensington, and Hazel quickly became the darling of London society. One simply could not throw a successful dinner party if one didn't invite John Lavery's exquisite new wife. And she *was* exquisite; John painted her over and over, but photographs show that he didn't exaggerate. Hazel had huge, soulful eyes that people—especially male people—could drown in. While John painted the society ladies, their husbands wrote love poems to Hazel. In 1918, John was knighted, and the couple became Lord and Lady Lavery.

Hazel had visited Ireland with John in 1913, and she fell in love with it. She started referring to herself as Irish instead of American, moved her birthday up to March 17, Saint Patrick's Day, and even managed to cultivate a slight Irish accent. Politics were bound to follow.

Hazel and John were converted to Ireland's cause on Easter 1916, when a few hundred rebels seized and occupied key buildings in Dublin. The Easter Rebellion was doomed from the start, though the small Irish army managed to hold out for a week. After the starving, tattered survivors surrendered, the British government executed sixteen rebel leaders, until an outraged public demanded they stop. The remaining rebels were sent to internment camps, and John Lavery donated a painting to a special benefit for the prisoners' families.

Three weeks later, John painted the trial of Sir Roger Casement. Hated England was at war with Germany, so naturally the Irish nationalists took Germany's side. Casement hatched a bizarre plot to sail to Germany and raise a battalion of Irish-born British soldiers being held there as prisoners of war. His mission was a disaster, and the Germans sent him back on a submarine. He landed on a beach in Ireland, where he was promptly arrested by the waiting British police.

He was tried in England for treason, and while John Lavery painted, Hazel attended the trial every day, lending her moral support to Casement. Casement noticed her, and wrote to his cousin: "Who was that lady who sat near the painter in the jury-box? . . . I thought I knew her face—it was very sad. . . . She had a wonderful face."

The trial reached its foregone conclusion: Casement was found guilty and hanged. Following the Easter Rebellion and the executions were five years of bloody war that the Irish call "the Terror." The Irish Republicans formed their own alternative government, Sinn Fein, and elected their own Parliament. England retaliated by sending in their military police, the infamous and brutal Black and Tans.

In 1920, when Terence MacSwiney, Lord Mayor of Cork, who'd been imprisoned by the British for treason, died after a seventy-four-day hunger strike, John painted his memorial service, attended by thousands of mourners.

Hazel, raised Episcopalian, converted to Catholicism.

Finally, after five years of bloodshed, England called for a truce, and invited a delegation from Ireland to discuss a treaty. Hazel and John opened their home to the Irish delegates, and John painted their portraits.

And Hazel fell in love with the leader of the delegation: Michael Collins, commander of the IRA, ruthless guerrilla leader, and inventor of modern urban warfare. Tall—they called him "the big fella"—and handsome, Michael Collins was a contemporary Cuchulain, an almost mystical figure. During the Terror, he had created an assassination squad known as "the twelve apostles," who, on one day, assassinated fourteen British officers. There was a £10,000 price on his head, yet the British had never even seen him.

Some of Collins's biographers, wishing their boy to remain true to his fiancée back home, insist nothing happened between Hazel and him, but evidence proves otherwise. They exchanged passionate letters, he wrote poems to her, and she was seen in public with him so many times that confused journalists described her as his "sweetheart."

John must have known. But he was thirty years older than Hazel, and in their terribly clever, terribly modern, and terribly rich circle, affairs were an accepted way of life. In fact, pretty, painted society ladies swarmed all over dashing, charismatic Collins, and he may also have had a brief affair with Lady Edith Londonderry. Edith's husband, Lord Londonderry, could hardly complain, since he had been Hazel's lover before Michael.

When he wasn't fighting off the ladies, Michael was suffering the torments of hell over the treaty. It was a compromise: Instead of becoming a republic, Ireland would gain a status similar to Canada's and would still have to swear allegiance to the crown. Collins knew there would be tremendous opposition in Ireland, but his only choice, between the treaty and many more years of bloodshed, was no choice at all. Hazel urged Collins to sign the treaty, and, dressed in her favorite opera cloak, drove him to 10 Downing Street to sign it. Afterward he phoned Hazel to tell her, "I have signed your damn treaty."

He also said, "I have signed my own death warrant."

He was right. Although a majority voted for the treaty, and Ireland became the Irish Free State, the country split into two factions. The resulting civil war saw friends fighting friends, brothers fighting brothers. On August 22, 1922, Michael Collins was assassinated.

John painted the hero on his deathbed. Hazel was inconsolable. She had to be kept from dressing in widow's black for the funeral; that honor belonged to Collins's fiancée, Kitty Kiernan. She tried to toss her rosary onto the coffin, but John retrieved it. Later, she had a friend insert the rosary under the glass pane that covered a wreath upon his grave.

Hazel carried Collins's letters around with her and mourned him for three years. Then she and Kevin O'Higgins, Vice President of the Irish Free State, fell in love. O'Higgins was married, so was Hazel; it didn't matter. John Lavery, perhaps getting tired of the way his wife, like Queen Maeve, always had one man in the shadow of another, took his wife on trips back to the United States, where he painted rich Americans. She hated the land of her birth, and she and Kevin resumed their relationship as soon as she returned.

In 1927 two things happened. First, John Lavery was commissioned to paint a portrait of a woman to symbolize Ireland, to appear on the country's new currency. He had already painted his wife as Roisin Dubh in a painting called "The Red Rose," which now hangs in the National Gallery of Ireland. In that one, Hazel is a queen dressed in dark red velvet, reclining in her thronelike chair. For the pound note, he portrayed her as Kathleen Ni Houlihan, a simple, though gorgeous, peasant girl draped in a traditional shawl. After 1976, Hazel stayed on the pound note in the form of a watermark, but today the Irish spend euros, and Hazel is gone.

The other thing that happened was that on July 7, Kevin O'Higgins, walking alone to church, was assassinated.

It was too much for Hazel. Every man she had ever loved (except for John, who would outlive her by six years) died before his time. It must be her fault; she must be cursed. She wrote to a friend:

> I am heartsick of all things Irish. . . . Everything that I dreamed and hoped and worked for lies in the dust.

As Hazel aged, her incandescent beauty faded. She spent hours at the mirror with her makeup and surrounded herself with pretty young men. Never strong, she developed a heart condition and took to her bed. John painted her there, in 1934, gaunt but still beautiful, reclining beneath a canopy of lace. He never completed the painting. She died in her sleep on January 3, 1935. On January 5, John painted his last portrait of Hazel—a picture of her coffin, draped with a cloth and covered with flowers. He titled it, "It Is Finished."

THE GIRL HE LEFT BEHIND HIM

Catherine Bridgit Kiernan, known as Kitty, born in Wicklow and convent educated, was not quite as gorgeous as Julia Roberts, who played her in the 2000 film, *Michael Collins,* but she was pretty enough to attract the big fella. She met Collins in 1917, when he and his friend Harry Boland stayed at her family's hotel. The two friends both courted Kitty, but she chose Michael, and before he left for London and the treaty negotiations, the two became engaged.

Ironically, Harry Boland, the man she turned down in favor of Collins, took the anti-treaty side, and was also killed during the second month of the civil war.

In 1925, Kitty married Felix Cronin, Quarter Master General in the Irish Army. They had two sons, and named the younger one Michael Collins Cronin. John Lavery had given her a portrait he painted of Michael, and it remained on her wall all her life. Felix Cronin must have understood.

She died in 1945, and was buried in Dublin's Glasnevin Cemetery, where Collins also lies.

Still Warriors after All These Years

Countess Markievicz

They called her "the Red Countess."

If Maud Gonne and Hazel Lavery personified Kathleen Ni Houlihan, and if Michael Collins was a twentieth-century Cuchulain, Countess Markievicz has to have been a reincarnation of the ancient warrior queen, Maeve.

Born in 1868, Constance Gore-Booth grew up with her sister in Sligo. Their mansion home, Lissadell House, had belonged to her family since the early seventeenth century. Rich and beautiful—she made her debut at the court of Queen Victoria, and was dubbed "the new Irish beauty"—she could have had and done anything she wanted. Like her friend Maud Gonne, what she wanted was to be a rebel, and what she did was shock proper Anglo-Protestant society.

Constance's first act of rebellion, in 1898, was to fall in love with Polish Count Casimir Markievicz, who was not only an artist (so was she) and a Catholic, but was already married. His wife conveniently died a year later, and in 1900 Casimir and Constance, already pregnant with their daughter, married, and she became Countess Markievicz.

Countess Markievicz.

The couple moved to Dublin and hung with the bohemian crowd. Constance already knew Yeats, who had visited her at Lissadell. It was inevitable that she would get interested in nationalist politics. She joined Maud Gonne's suffragist group, the Daughters of Erin, and wrote socialist articles for the organization's magazine. She joined Sinn Fein, the Irish separatist political party, and was elected to its council in 1909. That same year, she founded Fianna Eireann, an Irish militant version of the Boy Scouts, except that the boys practiced with rifles.

And in 1910, she was arrested for burning a British flag. All in all, Constance would wind up in the slammer for revolutionary acts at least five times more.

All of this was a bit much for Casimir, who joined the Imperial Russian Cavalry and split for the Balkans. Constance didn't miss him much. She was too busy fighting for Irish freedom.

By 1916 she had become the most militant of all the women in the movement for independence. That Easter, when a small citizen army of about a thousand people took Dublin, occupied major buildings, and held out for a week, Constance was second in command of one of the contingents. She marched at the head of the invading army, splendid in a green uniform she had designed herself: knee breeches and a belted tunic, a feathered hat on her head, a gun belt across her shoulders, and a rifle in her hand.

At the last minute, Constance had realized that the army needed a flag, so she made one from her green tablecloth. Finding herself almost out of gold paint, the countess thinned her paint with mustard, and printed "Irish Republic" on the banner. When a contingent of the army invaded the main post office, they flew Constance's flag from the roof.

Other women took part in the Easter Rebellion, but most of them were nurses and messengers, and they wore civilian clothes. Constance was one of only two women who wore a uniform and carried a gun—and used it, too. The rebellion was only a few hours old when she shot her first British soldiers.

The other uniformed woman was twenty-three-year-old Margaret Skinnider, who fought under the countess. Like the countess, Margaret was a crack shot, but at one point during the fighting, she was wounded by British soldiers. Constance held her hand as a doctor probed for the bullets. Satisfied the Margaret would be all right, she grabbed her gun and disappeared, returning to tell Margaret, "You are avenged, my dear."

The rebellion was a disaster. The small citizen army had expected similar uprisings all over Ireland, but due to dismal communications, they never happened. After six days, badly outnumbered and with the city a smoking ruin around them, James Connolly, the commander general of the troops, wounded and in great pain, gave the order to surrender. Constance objected. "Let's die at our posts," she suggested.

The British officer who accepted the army's surrender offered the countess a ride to prison. She was, after all, a woman, and he was a proper Edwardian. But she refused, preferring to march at the head of her troops, and march she did. Along with seventy other women prisoners, she was transferred to the women's prison, where she sat in solitary confinement, listening to the gunshots outside her window as the rebellion's leaders were executed, one by one.

Constance, as one of the leaders, was also sentenced to death, but her sentence was commuted because she was a woman. Infuriated, she said, "I wish your lot would shoot me."

Constance was pardoned in 1917, immediately resumed her work for the revolution, and converted to Catholicism. Readers who think of Catholicism today as one of the more conservative religions need to realize that for these women, Catholicism symbolized solidarity with the oppressed Irish, while Protestantism stood for the British ruling class.

By 1918, Constance was back in prison. This time, while in prison, she ran for Parliament on the Sinn Fein ticket and was elected, making her the first woman to be elected to British Parliament. Of course, since she refused to take an oath of allegiance to the king, she never took her seat. By the time she was out of jail again, Ireland had formed its own government, the Dail Eirann, and made Constance their labor minister. Of course, England considered it an illegitimate government, and the Dail members, including the countess, had to go into hiding, with prices on their heads.

In 1922, after Michael Collins signed the compromise treaty with England, Constance walked out of the Dail in protest, as did Dail President Eamon deValera and most of the other women members. Furious at Collins, the countess, who would never compromise, called him a traitor. He responded by calling her the worst thing he could think of: "English."

During the civil war that followed the treaty signing, Constance, by now in her mid-fifties, was arrested, along with Maud Gonne, by the Irish Free State. With ninety-one other women, the two staged a hunger strike and were released in a month. No matter how much they disagreed, the new Irish government, which counted William Butler Yeats among its senators, wasn't going to be responsible for the deaths of Ireland's two most famous firebrands.

She never stopped. In 1927, when Eamon deValera formed a new nationalist party, Fianna Fail, Constance ran for office and was elected. But the Red Countess had worn herself out, and on July 5, 1927, she died. Three hundred thousand people attended her funeral.

Three months later, Yeats remembered her in a poem called "In Memory or Eva Gore-Booth and Con Markievicz." He describes the sisters in their youth, dressed in silk kimonos, sitting at the tall windows of Lissadell. Both are beautiful, he writes, but one is "a gazelle." The gazelle was Constance.

AISLING POETRY 101

So who were these women—the Shan Van Vocht, Roisin Dubh, and Kathleen Ni Houlihan? To find the answer, let's take a course in Aisling.

Aisling—the word means vision or dream—was a new style of poetry and song, written in Gaelic, and popular in eighteenth-century Ireland. It followed a strict convention: the poet walks out on a May morning, or perhaps in midsummer, to breath the pleasant air, to see the lovely flowers, or to hear the birds sing. There on a hillside, or beneath a tree, or sitting on a rock by the ocean, he meets a fair maiden. Sometimes he falls asleep beneath the tree or on the hillside, and *dreams* that he sees the maiden. There follows a description of her: skin white as the lily, lips red as berries, golden hair rippling to her feet. But she laments for her lover who is over the sea, or her king who has left her alone. Sometimes she is dressed like a queen, sometimes she wears rags, but when her kingly lover returns, says the maiden, she'll wear a golden crown.

All very melancholy and romantic, but there was more to it than met the eye. The songs were code, and everyone knew what they meant. The fair maiden was Ireland herself, reduced to rags by the oppressive British rule. Sometimes the lover across the sea was Bonnie Prince Charlie, who tried to take back the throne from the British, failed miserably, and fled to France. It didn't matter that Charlie was Scottish; the Irish had always felt that the enemy of their enemy was their friend. Besides, he was Catholic.

And sometimes the lost lover or king was simply a symbol of Ireland's freedom, and the woman, instead of being a fair maid, was an ancient crone. But when her king returned, she would be made young and beautiful again:

Think her not a ghastly hag, too hideous to be seen . . .
Young she is, and fair she is, and would be crowned a queen,
Were the king's son at home here with Kathaleen
Ny-Houlahan!

Yes, the fair maid is Kathleen Ni Houlihan, and the ghastly hag is the Shan Van Vocht, the poor old woman, a symbol of Ireland made wretched and fallen upon hard times. There's more to the Shan Van Vocht, too, for she's another name for the ancient hag of Irish myth, the Cailleach. In Celtic myths, three brothers, some-times three princes, are camped in a forest, where they're approached by a hideous old woman who asks them for a kiss.

Two brothers shun her and make fun of her, but the third brother takes pity on her and kisses her—sometimes he does more than that!—whereupon, as in the song, she becomes a beautiful young woman, and bestows kingship on him.

Or the fair maiden is Roisin Dubh, meaning "Dark Rosaleen" or the "little dark rose"

> *Woe and pain, pain and woe,*
> *Are my lot, night and noon, To see your bright face clouded so,*
> *Like to the mournful moon.*
> *But yet . . . will I rear your throne*
> *Again in golden sheen;*
> *'Tis you shall reign, shall reign alone,*
> *My Dark Rosaleen!*

The women in these poems bore other names, too, but the names that stuck were the Shan Van Vocht, Roisin Dubh, and Kathleen Ni Houlihan, so that more than a century later the Irish still understood what they symbolized. When the wounded James Connolly, a leader of the Easter Rebellion, awaited execution by the British, he was attended by a doctor who wanted to know: Was there anything he could do? Connolly replied, "I want nothing but liberty."

The doctor said, "You must go to the Shan Van Vocht for that."
Connolly understood, as any Irish person would have. It was
like saying, "You must go to the Holy Virgin Mary."

Mother Jones

Exactly when did Mary Harris, emigrant from Cork, Ireland, adopt the persona of Mother Jones, quintessential white-haired little-old-lady labor organizer and all around hellion? She doesn't say in her biography, and no one seems to know. But once upon a time, Mary, born on the traditional labor holiday, May Day 1830, descended from Irish revolutionaries, was a wife and mother, and before that, a teacher and a dressmaker.

But she lost her entire family—her husband, ironworker George Jones, and all four children—to a yellow fever epidemic in 1867.

The new widow went back to dressmaking, sewing for rich people in Chicago. Already she was noticing the contrast between the very rich and the poor. She writes:

> Often while sewing for the lords and barons who lived in magnificence on the Lake Shore Drive, I would look out the plate glass windows and see the poor, shivering wretches, jobless and hungry, walking along the frozen lake front.

In 1871, tragedy struck again. The great Chicago fire burned up Mary's home and all her belongings. Along with other refugees of the fire, Mary camped out in a church that had been thrown open to the public. Nearby was an old tumble-down building where the Knights of Labor, an early labor organization, held their meetings. She started spending her evenings there, and eventually she joined the group. By 1880, she had decided to dedicate her life to the labor movement.

But all this time, she was still Mary Harris Jones.

The first time we read of her being called "Mother Jones" is in 1891, when at the age of sixty-one she traveled to Virginia to help organize miners during a strike. The miners called her "Mother," and she called them her "boys." By then, she probably already dressed in her trademark little-old-lady costume of widow's black silk, with white lace at her neck and a proper lady's hat atop her gray hair. The sweet little granny was a force to contend with. As she once said, "I'm not a humanitarian, I'm a hell-raiser."

As late as 1930, the year she died, Mother Jones still wore her trademark Victorian wardrobe, even though nobody wore clothing like that anymore. You couldn't even buy an outfit like that in 1930, but, seamstress that she was, she probably made the clothes herself. It was her costume. Whether on purpose or not, Mary Harris turned herself into the Shan Van Vocht, the poor old lady, and the Cailleach, the crone goddess of ancient Ireland.

Working conditions in the mines and the factories were

horrendous. The miners awoke before dawn, stayed underground as long as fourteen hours, and dragged themselves home to their tarpaper shacks after dark, too tired to do anything but eat and fall into bed. They never saw daylight. Families lived in wretched huts built by the mine owners, for which they had to pay exorbitant rent. Often they weren't even paid in money, but in scrip, which they traded for food and clothing at the company store. In constant debt to the mine owners, they were slaves in all but name.

Saddest of all were the children. Although there were laws against kids under age twelve working in the mines, desperate parents were willing to swear that their ten-year-old boy was twelve. Only boys who had lost an arm or leg in a mine accident went to school.

The fabric mills were just as bad. Kids as young as six and seven worked alongside their parents, for 10 cents a day. The exhausted children worked for twelve-hour shifts, falling asleep at their places on the line, losing fingers and hands—and sometimes lives— in the machines.

Mother Jones had the following pathetic conversation with a new mother who worked at one of the mills and thought she had a "good" boss:

"How old is the baby?"
"Three days. I just went back (to work) this morning. The boss was good and saved my place."

"When did you leave?"

"The boss was good. He let me off early the night the baby was born."

"What do you do with the baby while you work?"

"Oh, the boss is good and he lets me have a little box with a pillow in it beside the loom."

This 1903 cartoon from the New York *Evening Journal* compares Mother Jones with Long Island high society; high society comes out the loser.

In July 1903, Mother Jones brought the plight of child labor to the public eye by organizing a children's crusade. She marched about a hundred boy and girl mill workers, some missing fingers or entire hands, from Philadelphia through New Jersey to Oyster Point, New York, where then-President Teddy Roosevelt was vacationing, to demand child labor laws. The kids and seventy-three-year-old Mother Jones camped along the roadside or in the homes of sympathetic people. Farmers brought them fruits and vegetables to eat, and trains gave them free rides part of the way. The children's army marched through New York City, and on to Coney Island, where she lectured the audience at a wild animal show. Ever the showwoman, Mother Jones put the kids into empty animal cages.

"Fifty years ago there was a cry against slavery," she told the crowd, "and men gave up their lives to stop the selling of black children on the block. Today the white child is sold for two dollars a week to the manufacturers."

She pointed to a cage full of monkeys, and declared, "You see those monkeys in those cages over there, the professors are trying to teach them to talk. The monkeys are far too wise for they fear that the manufacturers would buy them for slaves in their factories."

When they reached Oyster Point on July 29, Teddy Roosevelt refused to see them. Always ready to milk any situation for what-

Another cartoon from Mother Jones's 1903 children's crusade shows the militia, all looking suspiciously like Teddy Roosevelt, preventing Mother Jones and her kids from entering his estate.

ever good she might get out of it, Mother Jones wrote the president a letter and sent copies to the newspapers.

The papers had a field day. Although the front pages of all the papers were dedicated to Pope Leo, who chose that particular week to die, Mother Jones made the second page. When she and her children arrived in New York City on July 23, the *Evening Journal* headlined, "Mother Jones Leads Army Into City." The *Philadelphia Evening Telegram* ran a cartoon depicting Teddy running away from the old lady. She says, "I see you, Mr. President," and the president says, "But I saw you first, Mother Jones."

Oddly enough, this radical who was called "the most dangerous woman in America" and "the grandmother of agitators" was not a suffragist. Maybe not so odd; she felt, erroneously or not, that the suffragists were spoiled rich women with no sympathy for the working class. I would have to put Mother Jones into the "I'm not a feminist, *but . . .*" category.

Because no matter how much she denied it, she was a feminist. She was famous for organizing "women's armies": armies of striking miners' wives armed only with mops, shovels, and tin pans. Banging on pie tins and howling like banshees, the women, with babies in one arm and brooms or mops in the other, would attack strikebreakers. "An army of strong mining women," she wrote, "makes a wonderfully spectacular picture."

During one of her women's army actions, Mother Jones struck up a conversation with the mining town sheriff. Not realizing who she was, he said, "Oh Lord, that Mother Jones is sure a dangerous woman."

Mother Jones asked, "Why don't you arrest her?"

"Oh Lord, I couldn't. I'd have that mob of women with their mops and brooms after me, and the jail ain't big enough to hold them all."

But once her women's army *was* arrested, for disturbing the peace. Mother Jones told them to bring their babies with them to court. When the judge couldn't hear himself for the howling of babies and asked if the women couldn't leave their kids home, they replied that miner's wives couldn't afford to keep "nurse girls."

They even brought their babies with them to prison. Mother Jones counseled the women in their cells to sleep all day and sing all night, which they did, loudly and raucously. The jailers complained, "These women howl like cats."

Mother Jones replied, "That's no way to speak of women who are singing patriotic songs and lullabies to their little ones."

Finally, nobody could stand the noise any more, and the women were freed.

Mother Jones herself was jailed countless times; once, when she was eighty-three, for conspiring to commit murder. Another time she was put under quarantine for smallpox. She took it in stride. During one of her periods in jail, she hooked up an "underground railway" to pass notes and even send telegrams: there was a hole in the floor of her prison cell, which she kept covered with a rug. When she signaled by knocking two beer bottles against each other, a friendly soldier would crawl under the building to receive the note she passed through the hole.

Where Mother Jones got her beer bottles from is another question.

She made it to one hundred. In fact, she made it to seven months after her hundredth birthday. More than 20,000 people showed up for her funeral. Irish to the end, her funeral was held at a Catholic church in Washington, D.C., but she was buried in the United Mine Workers Union Cemetery in Illinois with her "boys."

Mother Jones wouldn't have wanted anyone to waste much time in mourning. She had said, "Pray for the dead, but fight like hell for the living."

IRISH AMERICAN REBEL GIRLS

Mother Jones was not the only Irish American hell raiser. She had good company in two other women: Elizabeth Gurley Flynn and Margaret Sanger. Among the many things they had in common, all three were at one time members of the Industrial Workers of the World, commonly known as the I.W.W., or more commonly yet, as the Wobblies. The I.W.W. was probably the most radical labor union ever formed in America, advocating such "outrageous" ideas as the eight-hour workday and the forty-hour workweek. Both Mother Jones and Elizabeth Gurley Flynn were present at the founding convention of the I.W.W., in 1905.

Elizabeth Flynn was born in 1890 to a mother who had emigrated from Ireland in 1877. Like most immigrant families, Elizabeth's parents were poor and had too many mouths to feed, but Elizabeth had an advantage: both parents were socialists, and they gave their daughter a political education. At the age of sixteen, she gave her first public speech on socialism, and was arrested and expelled from school for it. This was only the beginning for her. Like Mother Jones, she became a union organizer and spent the rest of her life getting into trouble for good causes. A 1924 police report on Elizabeth lists her as having been arrested five times between 1906 and 1917.

In 1936, Elizabeth joined the Communist Party and proceeded to get herself arrested some more, especially in the McCarthyite 1950s, when she served two years in prison.

Elizabeth Gurley Flynn was a feminist and a founding member of the American Civil Liberties Union, the ACLU. She cut a dashing, romantic figure, and the writer Theodore Dreiser called her "an East side Joan of Arc." In 1915, songwriter Joe Hill, known as the troubadour of the I.W.W., wrote a song for her from his Utah prison cell, where he awaited execution on a trumped-up murder charge. It was called "The Rebel Girl":

That's the rebel Girl, that's the Rebel girl!
To the working class she's a precious pearl.
She brings courage, pride and joy
To the fighting Rebel Boy . . .
For it's great to fight for freedom
With a rebel Girl.

It would be hard to say which of the three women—Mother Jones, Elizabeth Gurley Flynn, or Margaret Sanger—seemed the most outrageous to people of their time, but I'd give my vote to Margaret Sanger. While the other two fought for an end to the grinding poverty of male and female workers, Margaret Sanger realized that the only way women could be really free of the cycle of poverty was to control the size of their families.

Margaret Louise Higgins was born in 1879, the sixth of seven children to Irish Catholic parents. Later she would say that her mother's early death, at the age of fifty, was partially due to her almost-constant state of pregnancy. Most certainly it was one reason why Margaret became a nurse.

In 1900, she married architect William Sanger, bore three children, and briefly tried out the traditional role of stay-at-home wife and mother, but conventionality was not for the likes of her. The family moved to New York City in 1910 and hung with the bohemian crowd in Greenwich Village. William took up painting, and Margaret went back to nursing. She also joined the Socialist Party and the I.W.W.

It was Margaret's work as a visiting nurse with the poor people of the Lower East Side that got her interested in family planning. She saw women physically and mentally broken by simply having too many children; she saw women dying in childbirth and from attempted self-abortions. By 1912, she was writing a column for the *New York Call* titled "What Every Girl Should Know." It dealt with what by today's standards is pretty tame stuff: personal hygiene, puberty, reproduction, and pregnancy, but when she wrote about venereal disease, the column was censored as "obscene."

Undaunted, in 1914, Margaret started publishing a monthly magazine called *The Woman Rebel*, advocating feminism and birth control. Within five months the magazine was banned, and Margaret was arrested for "sending obscene material through the mails." She jumped bail and split for England. While she was overseas, poor William was jailed for thirty days for distributing her sixteen-page birth control pamphlet, "Family Limitation," to an undercover agent.

Margaret sailed home to face the music on her *Woman Rebel* conviction, and when the charges were dropped, she embarked on a nationwide tour to promote birth control, getting herself arrested all along the way. In 1916, she opened the first birth control clinic. Nine days later, it was raided by the police, and she and all her staff were arrested. Margaret spent thirty days in prison for "creating a public nuisance."

In 1914, William and Margaret split up, and the sexually liberated Margaret spent the next few years having affairs with some pretty amazing men, like writers Havelock Ellis and H. G. Wells. She married again, in 1922, to millionaire James Slee, but this time with the understanding that, like Queen Maeve, Margaret would always have one man in the shadow of another. A year before her second marriage, she had founded the American Birth Control League, which eventually morphed into Planned Parenthood.

Today it's hard to believe that, simply for insisting that women had the right to regulate childbearing, Margaret was called lewd, vulgar, obscene, and immoral. To the Catholic Church, she was the devil incarnate. None of us would be the free women we are today without Margaret Sanger.

And a Single American Beauty Rose

Scarlett O'Hara

The fictional heroine of *Gone with the Wind* has become as mythic as Ireland's ancient warrior goddesses and queens, those heroines of *The Cattle Raid of Cooley*, but Scarlett O'Hara is the only one that you can see in a movie.

Biographies tell of how Scarlett's creator, Margaret Mitchell, raised in the South, learned all about the Civil War as a child. I believe her feminist mother, proud of her Irish Catholic heritage, must have also lulled little Margaret to sleep with tales of old Ireland. Certainly she knew her Irish history. In *Gone with the Wind*, Scarlett's father comes from a family of Irish rebels. He himself has fled to America after killing an English landlord, and he has named his plantation Tara, after Ireland's most sacred spot. Whether on purpose or subconsciously, Mitchell filled her all time bestseller with clues equating Scarlett with none other than Queen Maeve herself.

Maeve's saga and Scarlett's saga are both set against the backdrop of a great war, in which one side of a country battles the other side. And Mitchell didn't give Scarlett her name just because it's pretty. In ancient Ireland, red was the color of the warrior goddess, the Morrigan, and of all things magic. When the Morrigan

GONE WITH the WIND

BY MARGARET MITCHELL

Motion Picture Edition

★

appears to Cuchulain, disguised as a princess, she has red hair and red eyebrows, wears a long red cloak that drags on the ground behind her, and rides a red horse.

Within the limitations of the Old South, Scarlett is a warrior queen. In fact, she's queen of Tara. Not allowed to physically fight (although she *does* shoot a drunken Yankee soldier), she protects Tara in whatever way she can, even when it means tricking her sister's fiancé into marrying Scarlett instead. Maeve, who promised her own daughter to whomever would fight Cuchulain for her, also had no compunction against fighting dirty.

Cattle was so important in ancient Ireland that the worst crime an invader could commit was to destroy his enemy's cows. The Cattle Raid of Cooley was fought over a bull. Ancient myths are full of fairy cows, white with red ears; in fact, any red and white animal was suspected of having fairy origins. So it's no coincidence that the cow Scarlett acquires on her voyage back to Tara after fleeing Atlanta is red and white.

The cow finds Scarlett, rather than the other way around. It emerges from the bushes as though it's been waiting for her. Maybe it was sent by the Sidhe. In fact, Scarlett's maid, Prissy, thinks the cow is a ghost and wants to leave it behind, but Scarlett knows that you don't refuse fairy gifts and brings it with them.

Like Maeve, Scarlett marries three times, but always has one lover—Ashley Wilkes—in the shadow of the others. Too bad she can never sleep with him, but that's more Ashley's choice than hers. Despite this one nod to propriety, Scarlett still scandalizes proper Atlanta society. When everyone, including Rhett Butler, believes that she and Ashley really *are* lovers, she wears a shockingly low-cut, form-fitting dress to Ashley's birthday party. The dress is green, Ireland's color. Margaret Mitchell also linked her heroine with that color by giving her green eyes. Even the famous dress she fashions out of drapes is green.

Maeve lost the war with Ulster. The South lost the Civil War, and Scarlett lost Rhett. And like Maeve, she returned to the place where she was queen, Tara.

So, what then? The question most often asked after most of America read Mitchell's all-time bestseller was, "Does Scarlett get Rhett back?" Margaret Mitchell wasn't telling, and had vowed to never write a sequel. A speeding taxi that took her life in 1949 ended any chance that she might change her mind.

But in 1981, two of Margaret Mitchell's nephews gave novelist Alexandra Ripley the green light to answer the question that was still on everyone's lips. *Scarlett,* Ripley's sequel to *Gone with the Wind,* was published in 1991. Despite an absolutely dismal made-for-TV adaptation, the book is not bad, although it's no *Gone with the Wind*—after all, what is? Alexandra Ripley takes Margaret Mitchell's driven heroine and drives her to Ireland, where she meets her Irish relatives and becomes "the O'Hara," chieftain of her clan. In Ireland Scarlett gets involved with the Fennian Brotherhood, an Irish revolutionary society named after Finn MacCool and his men, and with a cailleach, an old witch woman. Oh yeah, and she gets Rhett back.

If I could rewrite *The Cattle Raid of Cooley*, I'd let Maeve keep the bull.

# FURTHER READING

If you want to read more about the women in this book, here's a good beginning reading list along with some helpful Internet sites. The following books are both fiction and nonfiction, and are in and out of print. Look for them in bookstores, at your library, and on the Internet.

Ancient Irish Goddesses and Warrior Queens

Clark, Rosalind. *The Great Queens.* Savage, MD: Barnes and Noble Books, 1991.

Monaghan, Patricia. *The Book of Goddesses and Heroines.* St. Paul, MN: Llewellyn Publications, 1990.

Monaghan, Patricia. *The Red-Haired Girl from the Bog.* Novato, CA: New World Library, 2003.

Women Pirates

Lorimer, Sara. *Booty.* San Francisco, CA: Chronicle Books, 2002.

Nelson, Pam, ed. *Cool Women.* Chicago, IL: Girl Press, 1998 (includes Mother Jones).

Women of the Irish Renaissance and the Easter Rebellion

Golway, Terry. *For the Cause of Liberty.* New York: Simon & Schuster, 2000.

Llywelyn, Morgan. *1916*. New York: Tom Doherty Associates, 1998 (a very good fictional account of the Easter Rebellion).

McCoole, Sinead. *Hazel: A Life of Lady Lavery*. Dublin, Ireland: Lilliput Press, 1996.

O'Connor, Ulick. *Michael Collins and the Troubles*. New York: W. W. Norton & Company, 1996.

Mother Jones

Gilbert, Ronnie. *Ronnie Gilbert on Mother Jones*. Berkeley, CA: Conari Press, 1993.

The autobiography of Mother Jones is in public domain and can be found on the Internet.
Try *www.eclipse.net/~basket42/mojones.htm*.

Irish Women in General

Diner, Hasia R. *Erin's Daughters in America*. Baltimore and London: Johns Hopkins University Press, 1989.

A highly recommended site on the Internet is Nancy Monaghan's *Famous Irish Women*,
http://www.geocities.com/pettigolass/
And of course:

Mitchell, Margaret. *Gone with the Wind*. New York: MacMillan Company, 1936.

INDEX

✤ about the author

Although she doesn't have a drop of Irish blood in her veins, Trina Robbins is a Celtophile who has traveled through Ireland, Scotland, Wales, and Brittany in search of ruins, graves, stone circles, and history—tramping through fields, stepping in cow pies, and getting chased out of meadows by herds of angry cows.

On her third trip to Ireland, she plucked a wild Irish rose from the slopes of Knocknarea, tomb of the warrior Queen Maeve, and placed it on the grave of William Butler Yeats, poet of the Celtic revival, friend of Lady Wilde, Lady Gregory, and Countess Markievicz, and ardent suitor of Maud Gonne.

Trina must have been Irish in a past life.